THE
STRUGGLE
TO BUILD
SOUTHEND'S
FIRST PIER

MARION PEARCE

Essex Hundred Publications

THE STRUGGLE TO BUILD SOUTHEND'S FIRST PIER
Marion Pearce

July 2025

A catalogue record for this book is available from
The British Library
ISBN 9781739931643

Typeset by Hutchins Creative

Printed by 4edge Publishing
22 Eldon Way
Eldon Way Industrial Estate
Hockley Essex SS5 4AD

Southend and the Thames Estuary in 1804

I

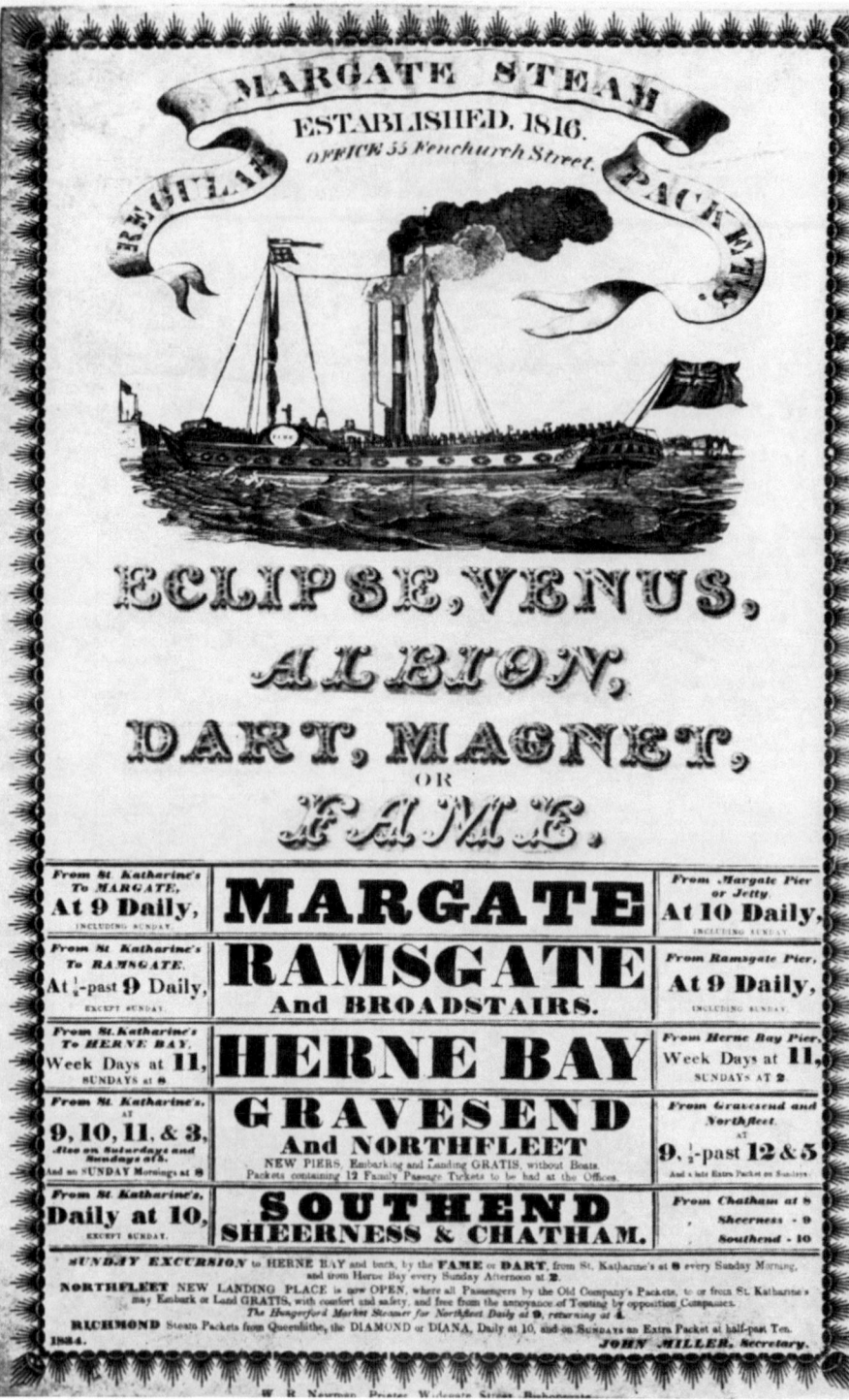

The Steam Packets 1834

CONTENTS

APPENDIX

LIST OF ILLUSTRATIONS

Cover Tide out Southend on Sea, remains of a 'hard' to deep water

Continued page 8

Continued from page 7

ERO   *Essex Records Office*
FOR   *Forum Southend*
SPM   *Southend Pier Museum*

ACKNOWLEDGEMENTS

Many people and organisations have assisted me in the research and writing of this book. Lord Rayleigh of Terling Place for supplying additional background material on General Goodday Strutt, Elaine Macgregor for giving details of the Vandervord fleet of Barges, the Forum Southend for access to period maps, the Southend Pier Museum, the British Newspaper Archives, the Essex Records Office and many other organisations for a variety of information or help.

With today's internet, many rare books and documents are now available online. This has been valuable in finding obscure facts about Southend Pier. I would also like to thank Andrew Summers, of Essex Hundred Publications, whose advice has been so valuable in the research and the editing of this book.

Marion Pearce

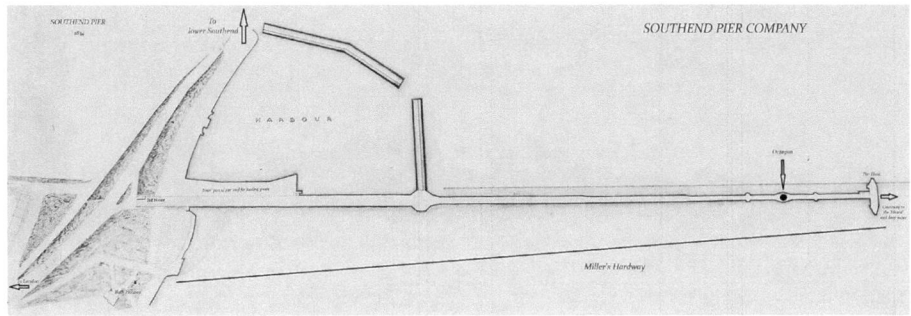

Plans of Southend's Pier Company's short pier released in 1834 showing the harbour, including landing wharf, the Octagon, Toll house, Shrubbery and Bath house and the track of Miller's hardway from the shore to the then pier head.

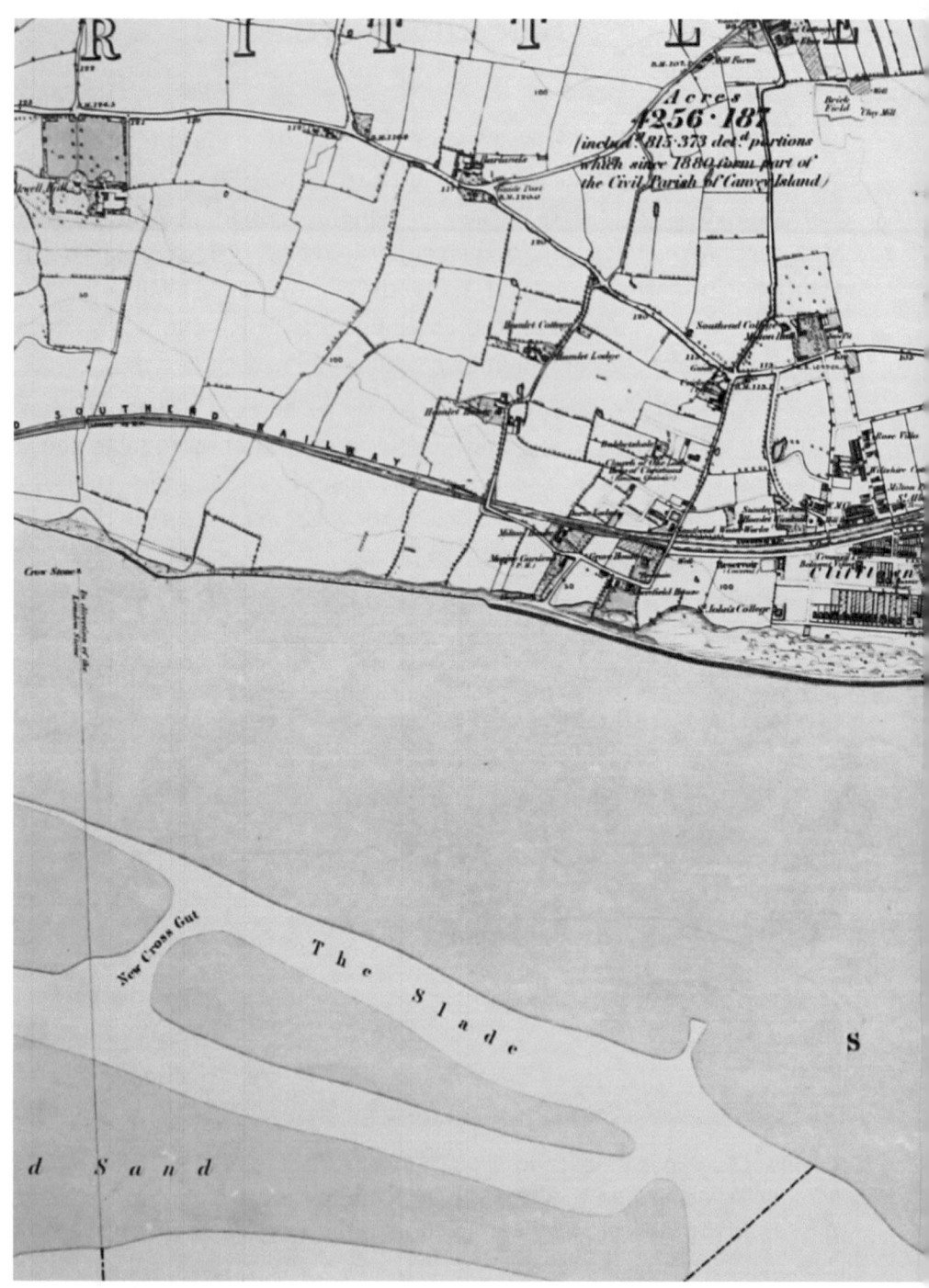

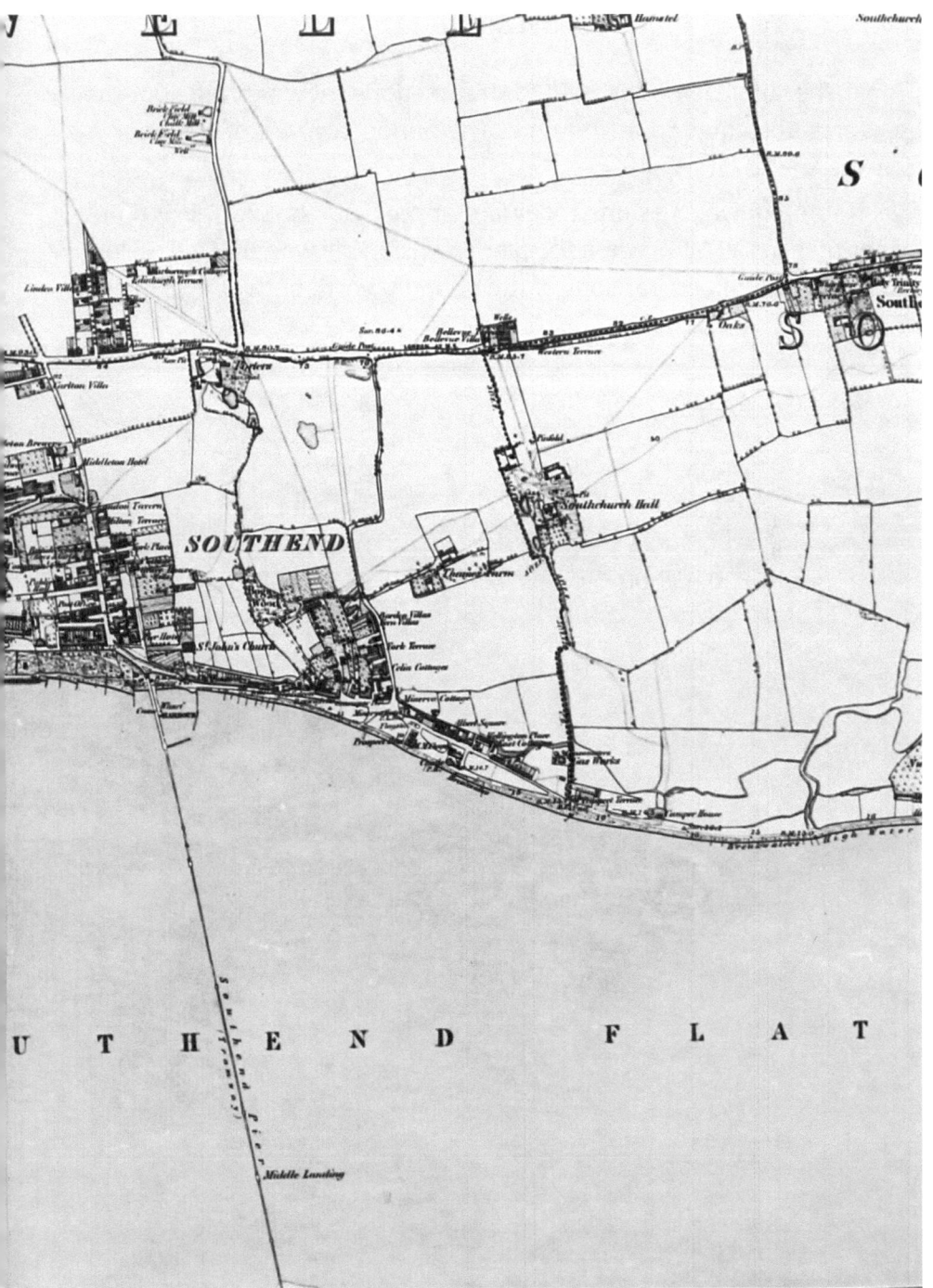

By 1877 Southend Pier had been extended to deep water. This map shows the centre of Southend and the railway line completed as far as central station.

INFLATION

The sums of money used for transactions shown throughout the book are those quoted at the time. The period covered of the book is from 1829 – 1875.

The equivalent sums today are approximately 170 - 190 times higher than in say 1835 when the pier extension bill was enacted. Below is a short table of comparisons of the pound's worth between 1835 and 2025.

1835		2025
£1.00	=	£162.00
£500.00	=	£81,184.08
£1,000.00	=	£162,368.00
£20,000.00	=	£3,247,363.06
1 shilling	=	£8.12

INTRODUCTION

There have been many books written about Southend Pier and its ups and downs during its history but this one is hopefully different as it outlines in detail the struggles to get the pier built in the first place.

In 1828 advertisements appeared in the local newspapers announcing that a local consortium intended to apply to Parliament to pass a bill to authorise the building of a pier in Southend. A year later, on March 13th 1829, an article appeared in the *Essex Chronicle* supporting the building of the pier in Southend.

The Struggle to Build Southend's First Pier covers the first 40 years of a remarkable story. Southend's pier is now more than 190 years old and is recorded as the longest pleasure pier in the world. Over its life span the pier has suffered several fires, severe damage from ships crashing into it and come close to being scrapped on grounds of cost by the local authority on more than one occasion.

From the early 1800s Southend was developing as a 'resort' town. Its fortunes were boosted firstly in 1801 when Princess Charlotte* of Wales, who was then five old, was sent to Southend on the recommendation of her doctors for sea bathing. She stayed at the *Lawn* in Southend. The trip had huge significance for Southend as Charotte was the heir-apparent to George IV and on his passing she would become Queen.

Three years after Charlotte's visit her mother Caroline Princess of Wales and the wife of the Prince Regent, visited Southend to take the waters. She stayed for six weeks.

Princess Caroline and her party occupied numbers 7, 8 and 9 of what is now Royal Terrace. The visit in turn attracted what might be called the 'fashionable' society to visit the town.

Yet, difficult access from London both by road and river hindered development. In the early 1800's the railways were yet to come. Southend, sited on the north shore of the River Thames as it emptied into the North Sea, had no natural harbour so there was nowhere onshore to disembark visitors when the tide retreated. Passengers destined for Southend had to be transferred from larger ships onto smaller vessels, rowed ashore and then when the tide was out walk, or be carried, the rest of the way across the mud.

Furthermore, business and civic leaders in Southend considered the town was losing out when Margate in Kent, which was further from the Pool of London than Southend, constructed a pier where passengers could disembark without getting their feet wet or muddy.

Thus, the solution for Southend was to build a pier of its own out into deep water to accommodate the growing number of larger ships plying the river. However, from the very outset the prospect of a pier being built in Southend was mired in argument. Powerful businessmen and landowners had different views as to where the pier should be built and who should pay for it. Some in 'fashionable' society who held property in Southend opposed the pier altogether as they believed it would spoil their sea view and that increasing numbers of visitors would be a nuisance. Fishermen and oystermen were alarmed at the prospect of their fishing grounds being irreparably damaged. The watermen who ferried goods and passengers from large ships to shore also feared for their survival.

There were multiple legal disputes between the parties which continued on and off for 10 years both during and after its erection. The possibility, let alone the imposition, of tolls for using the pier itself and subsequent tolling of the roads approaching the pier led to violence and riot. The pier toll gates and toll house were vandalised on more than one occasion. The local magistrates seemed powerless and were unable or unwilling to punish the offenders. The principal mover for building Southend Pier was William Heygate, a prominent resident, former Lord Mayor of London and a Baronet. He lived at *Porters* which later became the Southend mayor's house. He also had a house on Royal Terrace.

Heygate led a syndicate of supporters to promote the pier. Later the Southend Pier Company was floated and William Heygate became the chairman.

In turn the Pier Company was charged with managing all aspects of financing and building of the pier. The plan to build the pier gained Royal Assent on the 14th May 1829. A week later the foundation stone was laid. However, with the Parliamentary Bill came sweeping powers that sowed much of the discord that followed.

The other prominent family at the beginning of the pier story was the Vandervords. The Vandervords were shippers who owned a large fleet of barges and hoys**. They also had interests in farming and were corn merchants. The Vandervord family can be traced back to the 15th century but for the purposes of this book we begin with Abraham Vandervord who was born in 1759 in Leigh-on-Sea. He lived until 1817. Abraham was responsible for building the first short chain pier sited on Southend seafront, opposite where the Kursaal now stands, long before the present pier took shape.

Sadly, details of this pier are lacking. Abraham was the father of William Heard Vandervord, Mary Vandervord, James Wilson Vandervord, Mary Warrington Vandervord, George John Vandervord and two others whose names are not known. With Abraham Vandervord's death in 1817 his sons William, James and George took over running the business.

At the outset the Vandervord family, with some reservations, supported the proposal of Sir William Heygate to construct a new pier. Yet, disagreements with the Pier Company quickly arose after the Vandervords were given the impression that the new pier would primarily be used for the unloading and shipping of the Vandervord's, or their customer's goods and also that it would be built where the original chain pier stood in lower Southend. However, William Heygate denied this was ever the case. The Vandervords were particularly aggrieved at the levels and scope of the tolls envisaged and consequently the family instructed their agents and barge captains to refuse to pay them. They later sponsored a petition to parliament opposing the financing and extension of the pier to deep water. This action drew widespread support from farmers, fishermen, watermen and other landowners in Southend.

However, there was discontent within the ranks of the Pier Company too. General Wiiliam Goodday Strutt, an old soldier and a key board member, was worried about the pier finances from the outset.

He objected to how the Pier Company dealt with opposition to the project and was also unhappy with his fellow board members as they repeatedly ignored his advice and left him out of crucial decision making.

The disputes with the Vandervords continued well into the late 1830s but even when they were seemingly settled, a whole new set of challenges emerged. Yet, despite the ongoing legal disputes and the petition to parliament opposing the pier, construction continued, eventually reaching deep water. The first pier was made from wood and was nearly one and a quarter miles long.

Following this narrative there is an appendix starting on page 83. It has details of the original shareholders, the pier specification and extracts of the transcript of the principal court case connected with enforcing tolls. Additionally, there is a précised transcript of the meeting of Southend ratepayers to argue out the case to buy the pier for Southend, some sample letters and the application for the parliamentary enabling bill.

So, step back in time and enjoy the remarkable story of the struggle to build Southend's pier. Based on a wealth of material taken from contemporary newspaper and court reports together with extracts of the minutes of key meetings and years of research, *The Struggle to Build Southend's First Pier* comes to life.

At the same time, we learn about the many colourful characters involved that make up this amazing tale.

* Princess Charlotte of Wales died in childbirth aged 21. The baby was stillborn. Her death altered the Royal succession and in turn led to Victoria, aged 18, becoming the Queen in 1837.

** A list of the Vandervord family barges (where known) with available detail added is shown in the appendix No 3 from page 87

THE CASE FOR BUILDING THE PIER

The mid-19th century was the golden age of building piers in British seaside resorts. Yet, building a pier was no simple task. Before any construction could begin parliamentary approval was needed. Local landowners had to be persuaded to sell or lease land to enable access to the pier. Fishermen and watermen had to be consulted as pier construction and its siting could interfere with fishing grounds and tidal flows. The River Thames was the principal commercial route into London so approval from the Admiralty and Trinity House (which had responsibility ensuring maritime safety) was needed. Thus, getting agreement from several parties, sometimes with different agendas, was time consuming and expensive. It required delicate negotiations. All the while much capital had to be raised to finance the pier's construction.

In the early 1800's, Southend was becoming a thriving, fashionable holiday and bathing resort, where spending time by the sea and the taking the airs was deemed to have considerable health benefits. *The Essex Herald* of Tuesday *of* 15th September 1829, said of Southend: "This much-admired watering place has been this season visited by an unusual number of families of distinction. This truly desirable and healthy retreat, so happy in its situation and local advantages, and so salubrious in its atmosphere shall be rendered inferior to none in the kingdom for its comfort and convenience."

A long list of members of the aristocracy had visited Southend to take the airs. As already mentioned, perhaps the most famous visitor to Southend was Princess Caroline of Wales, the wife of the Prince Regent. Later, in 1834 the Earl of Beaconsfield (then Mr. Benjamin Disraeli the future Prime Minster) sojourned at Porter's Grange and is credited with having described Southend as the Riviera of Essex. The writer and poet Robert Buchanan, who is buried St John's Baptist Church in Southend, made several visits to Southend and later he and his wife Mary set up home on Cliff Town Parade. Mary was in poor health and it was thought Southend's sea air would retore her health.

As Southend was the closest seaside town to the capital, the pier's advocates hoped more Londoners (apart from the very rich and famous) would come to Southend if access could be improved.

Before the pier and the railways, for visitors who arrived at Southend from London, after sailing down river or later coming by the new Thames steamers, to get ashore was time consuming and difficult at the best of times. The Southend coast consists of mudflats extending far from the shore, with a high tide depth seldom exceeding 5.5 metres (18 ft). Medium sized ships could only dock at short jetties during high tide. Ships with deep keels had to remain in deep water and no boats could approach the jetties at low tide. At low tide travellers needed to transfer not only themselves from large ships to small boats, but also their baggage. There then followed the prospect of trekking across a muddy shore and beach to dry land in all weathers.

A Southend Pictorial Telegraph cartoon published in 1936 drawn by Fred Naughten. Naugton was a bit of a history buff. He drew many cartoons from times past. This image shows the view from the shore in Southend before any pier was built and steamers bypassing Southend on their way to Herne Bay or Margate. It is believed the steamer closest was the Regent that began a regular service to Margate shortly after 1816.

For overland journeys from London, before the railways were built, travel was also difficult as the roads were rough and often muddy which limited travel speeds. There was no street lighting and robbers and bandits were frequently lying in wait for the unwary. The trip from London to Southend would likely take a full day by horse-drawn carriage as the horses required frequent rest stops. John Burrows, the Essex historian, in his 1908 *Southend-on-Sea Historical Notes* gives an account of the Lord Mayor of London's trip to Southend. "The Lord Mayor of London, Slingsby Bethell MP set out at six in the morning in his coach from the Mansion House and arrived around six in the evening at Leigh-on-Sea".

Another of Fred Naughton's cartoons drawn in the 1930s illustrates the challenges of travelling by road from London to Southend before the railways came.

Another account of overland travel came from the preacher John Wesley who came from London to Leigh-on-Sea on 27th October 1755. He recorded a graphic description of his journey in his diary.

"We set out for Leigh, in Essex, but being hindered a little in the morning, the night came on, without moon or stars, when we were two miles short of Rayleigh.

The ruts were so deep and uneven that the horses could scarce stand, and the chaise was continually in danger of overturning; so that my companions thought it best to walk to town, though the road was both wet and dirty. Leaving them at Rayleigh, I took horse again. It was so thoroughly dark that we could not see our horses' heads; however, by the help of Him to Whom the night shineth as the day, we hit every turning, and without going a quarter of a mile out of our way, before nine we came to Leigh". Again, it had taken all day for Wesley to travel from London to Leigh on Sea.

Once access to Southend was improved by building the pier there were other economic and financial benefits that William Heygate was keen to bring to the town. With many potential visitors sailing further down river to Herne Bay or Margate on the Kent coast, Southend was losing out. Both the Kent towns had built piers and were reaping a good harvest from a growing amount of steamboat traffic. Naturally Heygate didn't want Southend to suffer from the competition and this in turn reinforced his case for Southend to have a pier of its own.

Besides the increase in passenger traffic the pier would bring benefits to local agriculture. Southend and Essex Farmers would be able to ship their produce more efficiently, especially to London. A solid pier would offer protection for shipping in rough weather and give cover for farmers' wagons and horses whilst they waited to load or unload. Improved communications between Essex and Kent were as also seen as another pier benefit. The huge naval and military works at Sheerness generated much cross-estuary river traffic.

The *Essex Herald* of the 17th March 1829 added, "During Mutiny at the Nore, every military and naval man contacted lamented the want of a Pier.

The Duke of York, in his survey of the Coast, thought it desirable, and Captain Beaver, that excellent and skilful commander of the Coast Fencibles, wrote to Government to advocate the measure".

In 1814 a small steam packet called *The Thames (*designed by Brunel*)* arrived in Margate from St Katherine's Dock, near the Tower of London. The arrival sparked fierce hostility from local watermen. A year later this ship was replaced by a larger ship called the *Regent.* The *Regent* was in turn replaced by a series of larger and larger vessels and by 1819 a regular service from London along the River Thames was in operation with some ships serving Southend, tide permitting. However, Margate's steamer trade was substantially boosted when a new jetty was built that allowed passengers to land in comfort and during the 1825 season over 50,000 passengers went to Margate.

Southend was now at a considerable disadvantage compared to her Kent rivals. The town was losing out. A deep-water pier would take advantage of the rapid extension of the new steam navigation along the Thames where "A more commodious landing of passengers and goods will give Southend an increase of trade, importance, and property". So, the inconvenience, delay, and damage arising from the lack of a pier was obvious.

Although the pier would bring many benefits to industry, agriculture and the wider community in Southend-on-Sea, the venture was not a charitable venture on the part of William Heygate and his consortium. The consortium hoped the pier would be a revenue earner over time through tolls and dues levied on users of the pier. The consequential increase in the number of visitors to Southend would also boost revenue for the businesses and inflate land values that consortium members had interests in. The consortium minutes recorded,

"There was also a possibility of obtaining revenue from the use of the pier by residents and visitors. A new promenade could be built and attractions increased by such an amenity – the pier".

Southend Pier was the first long pier built on the Essex coast. Although Walton-on-the-Naze Pier initially opened in 1830 it wasn't until 1848 that it was extended to just 350 feet. In contrast, by September 1830 Southend Pier was already 600 feet long. Clacton Pier was built between 1870 and 1871.

Already mentioned in the introduction and it is worth repeating; the case for Southend-on-Sea's Pier was neatly summed up by the *Essex Chronicle* of March 13th 1829, (see also page 13).

"It is remarkable that along the line of coast of the County of Essex, reckoning from Tilbury Fort to Harwich, an extent of nearly 100 miles, there does not exist a single harbour or landing place at which it is practicable to land passengers or goods with safety and convenience at low water."

The view from Lower Southend to the Royals, shortly after their completion in 1800, where the Heygates also owned property.

THE PIER COMPANY AND PIER CONSORTIUM

Following the third reading of the Pier Act (May 1829, also known as the *Southend Pier and Improvement Bill)*, Sir William Heygate formed the Southend Pier Company. The members of the company were drawn from the syndicate set up earlier. In its short existence the syndicate had been busy; it had drawn up plans, lobbied parliament and consulted interested parties on the pier project.

The Pier Company capital was fixed at £12,000 and divided into 240 shares of £50 each. The first general meeting of shareholders was called by public advertisement and reported in the *Essex Herald* on Tuesday 2nd June 1829 as being held in the Bank Coffee House, Cornhill in London. A list of known shareholders can be seen in the appendix page 83.

The company's purpose in broad terms was to construct a pier and to have the right to levy tolls on water-carried merchandise landed on the foreshore three miles on either side of the *Ship Inn.*

Additionally, the "Southend Pier Company had responsibility for maintaining at the extremity of the pier, a good and sufficient light under regulations laid down by the Corporation of the Trinity House", the body that regulated traffic on the River Thames.

The *Herald* continued "At this first meeting from a special committee of prominent local men the Pier Company was formed. Appointed to the board, were the following Gentlemen, **Sir Thomas Maryon Wilson, Bart.**, **Major-General Strutt, J. W. Heygate Senior, J. Heygate, Junior, George Greaves, J. Finlay, and D. Smith. R. Greenward,** a banker of Chelmsford, was appointed Treasurer and **E. Mackmurdo**, a London Solicitor, as Clerk to the Company. **William Heygate** was elected as chairman".

However, the principal parts in this important syndicate were taken by the Heygate family and General Strutt. The Heygates were wealthy bankers and landowners and the Strutt family were influential in the Chelmsford area and also with the Crown and Parliament.

William Heygate, the principal advocate of building the pier, perhaps in the day, in Southend, could have been called 'Mr Pier'.

Sir William Heygate around 1822

William Heygate was the first son of James Heygate senior, a London banker who had made large purchases of land in Southend which included the manor house of *Porters* and a wide area around it.

Porters in turn became the Heygate family home in Southend, although the family also owned property elsewhere in Southend, in London, Leicestershire, Staffordshire and Derbyshire. William was born on 24th June 1782. Two years later his brother James junior was born. Following his formal education William joined his father in the banking business. He was prominent in City affairs for over thirty years and a member of the Worshipful Company of Merchant Taylors.

William was also active in London politics and became a Common Councillor in 1809 for the curiously named ward of Cripplegate Within.

In his role as a Common Councillor William was able to play a valuable part in the running of the Square Mile.

In 1812 he was elected Alderman for Coleman Street Ward, an office he held until his death in 1843. He was also Sheriff for the year 1811-12, Lord Mayor of London in 1822-3 and later the City Chamberlain.

William Heygate's name appeared on the north face of the smaller Crowstone in Chalkwell following his ceremonial visit that year. The name was later added to the east face of the newer taller Crowstone which still stands on the seafront at Chalkwell.

Between 1818 and 1826 William Heygate served as the Tory Member of Parliament for Sudbury. Yet he frequently took an independent line in voting for tax, parliamentary and criminal law reform. He pressed in vain to have a three-year restriction on the 1819 blasphemous libels and seditious meetings bills.

Heygate also thought it was a mistake to prosecute Princess Caroline of Brunswick, (the Princess of Wales) the estranged wife of the King George IV, in what became known as 'The Queen Caroline Affair,' which saw the Queen put on trial in the House of Lords charged with adultery.

Following his term as Lord Mayor of London, William Heygate sent a request to the Prime Minster, Lord Liverpool, to be honoured with a Baronetcy. However, this was turned down, partly on account of the precedent it might set and perceived tensions between the city and the king. In 1929 his application was again turned down by the then Prime Minister, the Duke of Wellington. Nevertheless, his wish was granted two years later, in 1831, as part of King William IV's coronation honours. Thus, William Heygate became Southend's first Baronet and was entitled to use the term William Heygate Bart on official inscriptions.

William Heygate married Isabella Mackmurdo in May 1821. The union produced four sons including Frederick William Heygate, born in 1922, followed by William Unwin Heygate in 1825. Today Heygate Avenue in Southend remains and a diesel pier train bearing the name *Sir William Heygate* came into service in May 1986. The *Sir William Heygate* was replaced by a new electric trains in 2022 but remains in service as a reserve train for the time being.

There was no doubt that William Heygate's contacts in the city and parliament were of great help in bringing the parliamentary bill to fruition and thus enabling the building and financing of Southend Pier.

The other leading figure on the consortium was **General William Goodday Strutt**. It should also be highlighted that without the general's surviving comprehensive letter-books much of the early story of Southend Pier would not be known.

William Goodday Strutt was born in 1762, the second son of John Strutt of Terling Place, Essex, now the home of successive Lords of Rayleigh. Strutt was educated at Felsted School. Aged 16, Strutt joined the army as an ensign in the 61st Regiment of Foot. He soon saw active service in the War of American Independence and later was present at the 1782 siege of Gibraltar. He subsequently fought with distinction in the French Revolutionary war in Flanders and later in the West Indies. In 1795, having been promoted to the rank of Brigadier-General, he was sent to the West Indies for the third time and to the island of St Vincent during the second Carib war. On the 8th January 1796, in a fierce engagement, he was wounded three times* which resulted in the loss of his right leg from just above the knee.

*General Strutt kept the musket ball that shattered his leg as a grim souvenir of the occasion. It was kept in a box at Terling Place labelled "The ball that shattered my leg".

General William Goodday Strutt in about 1810.
Unnamed artist from Witham

Goodday returned to England in May 1796. He was received by King George III who made him deputy Governor of Stirling Castle, a sinecure appointment. Despite having lost a leg Strutt hoped to return to active services but after an initial positive response from the Duke of York, the Commander-in-Chief of the Army, the request was turned down on medical grounds.

Strutt was alternatively offered the Governorship of Quebec and on 23rd June, 1798 he was raised to the rank of Major-General.

The governorship was another sinecure appointment. The post provided him with a salary but required little on his part. It was described as an appointment without responsibility, labour or service. He held the post until his death. The general said during the time he was governor he never visited Quebec.

Although Strutt's principal home was at 'Tofts' in Great Baddow, he had a fondness for the sea. In 1824 be built a house in Southend on what is today Marine Parade. The house was called *Rayleigh House*. Southend then was described as a "Comparatively unspoilt village".

General Strutt joined the Pier Consortium in 1829. Amongst his responsibilities when the Pier Company was formed was getting plans and drawings agreed, organising consultations and supervising the erection of the pier. Despite severe rheumatism in both hands, he was a prolific letter writer and as mentioned earlier the contents of his letter-books provide much insight into the early pier history.

When Strutt joined the Pier Company, he was not a well man. He was sixty-seven years of age, afflicted with gout, minus a leg, without most of his teeth and had a bullet in his body which doctors had been unable to extract. He died at Tofts, Little Baddow, Essex, on the 5th February, 1848, having given exceptional service both at home and abroad. *Rayleigh House* still stands but after Strutt's departure it was converted into a restaurant and later an amusement arcade. The stretch of pavement in front of the restaurant was once known as Strutt's Parade. Strutt's legacy also survives in Little Baddow in the form of a pub called the *General's Arms*.

Major - General William Goodday Strutt (1762 - 1848)

Entering the army in 1778, he served with various regiments & took an active role in a number of engagements. In 1794 he bore a very distinguished part against the French at Ticl, going through much hard fighting. On his return he was sent to St. Vincent. In January 1796, with two hundred men, he attacked a force of twelve hundred, being himself thrice wounded, & losing his right leg. On 13th May 1800 he was as a reward for his services, appointed govenor of Quebec. He died at Tofts, Little Baddow, Essex, on 15th February 1848.

A plaque on the outside wall at the General's Arms, Little Baddow

Another member of the pier company was **James Heygate Junior**. Heygate Junior was the younger brother of William Heygate. He was a director in the family business, the Alliance Marine Assurance Company, in London. However, he mainly made his money in the Leicester hosiery business. He also established, with Thomas Pares, *the Pares, Heygate & Co* bank. The bank did well initially, but around 1830 it fell into difficulties when it emerged that James Heygate had been embezzling funds. The incident caused much distress in the Heygate family. He resigned from the bank and most probably took temporary leave from the Pier Company too. Nevertheless, James Heygate junior bounced back. He lived with his family at Porters which he and his wife rented. In 1868 they raised sufficient funds to purchase the house, buildings and surrounding land. James Heygate junior also served as Chairman of the Southend Local Board (an early forerunner to Southend City Council) that eventually decided to buy the pier.

Edward Longdon Mackmurdo, a solicitor from Saint John, Hackney, Middlesex, was Clerk to the Southend Pier Company. He was the father of Isabella and Anna who respectively married William and James Heygate junior. The treasurer of the Pier Company was named in various letters as **R. Greenward, esq**. a banker of Chelmsford. One of the other baronets whose name cropped up in correspondence was **Sir Thomas Maryon Wilson.** Other company members given were **George Greaves, J. Finlay,** and **D. Smith**. Less is known of these Pier Company members. Newspaper reports of the day didn't give full details and company records are incomplete. Aged 82, **James Heygate Senior** was also a member of the consortium and subsequently became a Pier Company board member.

However, there is no doubt, from examination of the records available, **Sir William Heygate** and **William Goodday Strutt** (despite his age and disability) dominated the early days of the pier company.

CONSULTATIONS
The meeting at the Royal Hotel March 30th 1829

As the Pier bill passed through its final stages in parliament Sir William Heygate called a meeting of interested parties and stake holders to reveal more details of the pier plans and update them on progress. The reports of this meeting have been compiled from the *Essex Herald, The Essex Chronicle* and entries extracted from the Essex historian John Burrow's book *Southend Pier and its Story*. The meeting took place at the Royal Hotel on Monday March 30th 1829.

It was a key meeting held to get local consensus. Heygate considered this essential to move the pier project forward. The Royal hotel, built around 1790, was originally called the *Capital.* Following Princess Caroline, the Princess of Wales's, visit to Southend, the hotel was licensed as the Royal and its name was changed to the Royal Hotel. In its heyday, the hotel became the centre of social life with functions regularly frequented by leading society figures. It was described as the most expensive hotel in the town.

The first part of the meeting took place in the morning in the form of a quasi-judicial enquiry where witnesses were called.

The Royal Hotel and Library in about 1800.

Its purpose was to discuss the overall situation and gage the level of support. Already what was known about the pier plans had caused some disquiet particularly from the Vandervord family who, since 1770, had owned barges and had a weekly sailing from Southend to the Pool of London. Heygate told the attendees quiet bluntly "That, unless the pier proposal is met with general concurrence of the meeting, he would abandon it forthwith, notwithstanding the great personal expense and trouble to which he had been put".

At the root of the disquiet were the proposals for pier tolls and confusion as to where the pier should be sited. Doing the rounds was talk of "A promise made or implied that the pier should be situated at a point on the beach opposite Old Southend Road", (by the present day Kursaal building).

This statement was echoed by William Fox, a shopkeeper who had a draper's shop. He added that "A jetty was to be at a house called the *Laboratory* and the pier at Vandervord's Lane". As noted earlier Southend already had a short chain pier which consisted of chains suspended between wooden piles that had been constructed by barge owner Abraham Vandervord.

Abraham's son George Vandervord was present at the meeting and said, "The pier should be fixed in a fit and proper place". Sir William Heygate assured him it would be. Christopher Parsons, of Southchurch, a naturalist and diarist, said "He understood Sir William Heygate to say that the pier was to be at the old landing place – the Old Ship, nearly opposite Messrs. Vandervord's premises". George Vandervord then asked "When will it be seen that the pier was to be placed at the side of the jetty", to which Heygate was said to have replied, "Certainly there should be a safe and convenient place for vessels to land and discharge in all weathers".

The conversation seemed to imply two piers would be built, one where the present pier stands below the Royals and another loading pier by the Kursaal. Adding to the confusion and not helping matters was the fact that, despite various debates and scrutiny in parliament, "No pledge of a distinct site for the pier was given during the proceedings. The plans submitted gave limits on the seafront within which the pier or piers should be erected, but specified no particular site."

Continued page 34

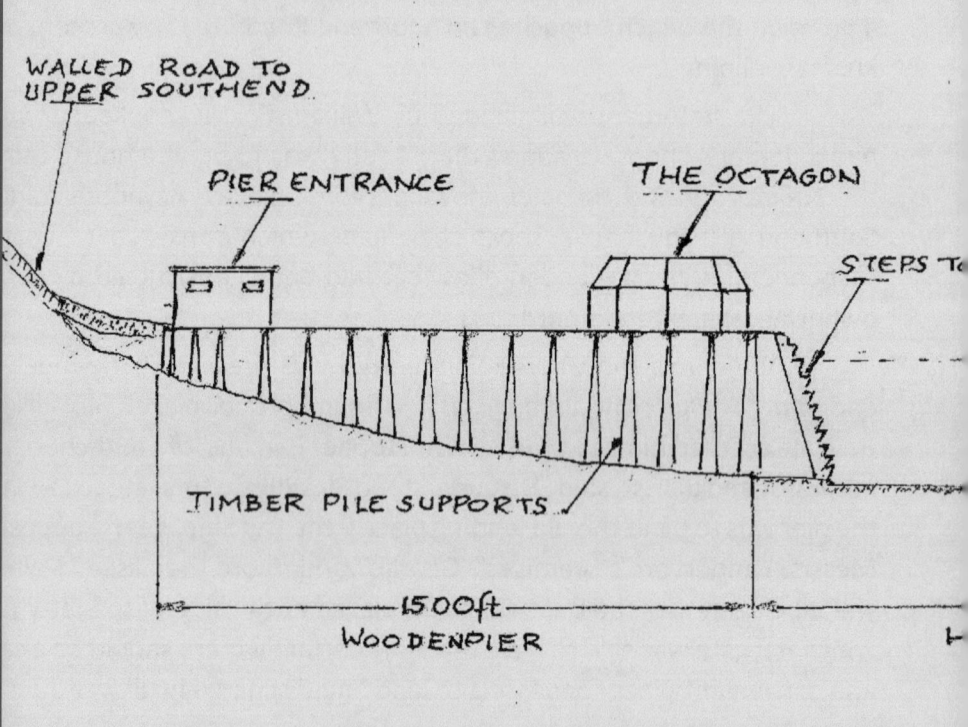

SOUTHEND PI
ILLUSTRATED SIDE
FROM THE

WALLED ROAD TO
UPPER SOUTHEND

PIER ENTRANCE

THE OCTAGON

STEPS T

TIMBER PILE SUPPORTS

1500ft
WOODENPIER

1835 (APPROX)
VATION
ST (NOT TO SCALE)

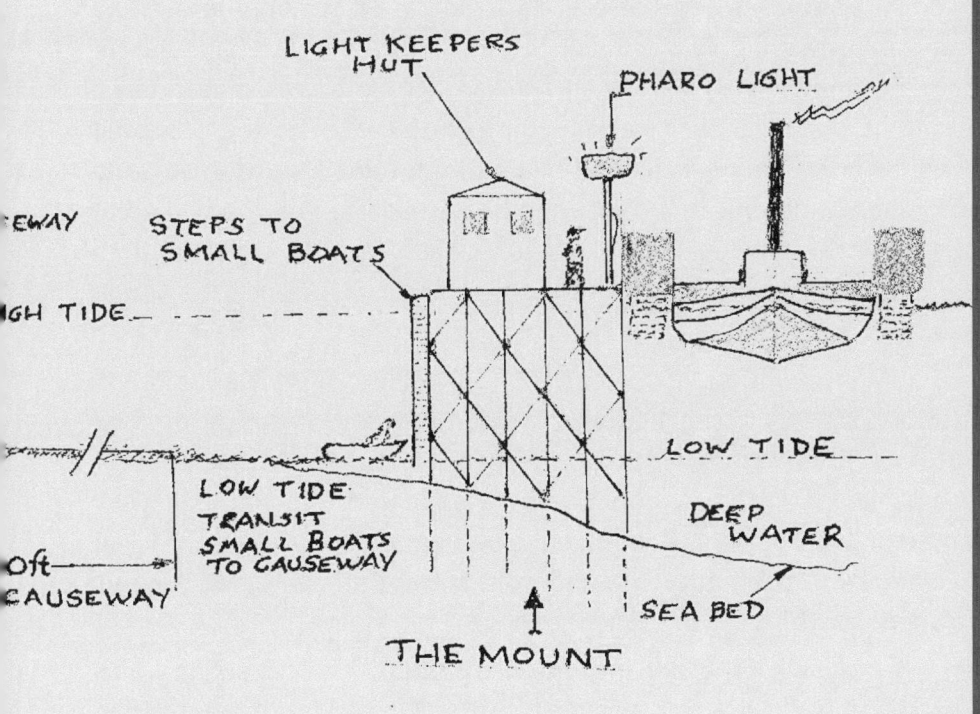

LIGHT KEEPERS HUT

PHARO LIGHT

EWAY

STEPS TO SMALL BOATS

GH TIDE

LOW TIDE

LOW TIDE TRANSIT SMALL BOATS TO CAUSEWAY

DEEP WATER

Oft CAUSEWAY

SEA BED

THE MOUNT

Continued from page 31

It seems that at this point the meeting became very stormy but nevertheless Sir William Heygate managed to assure George Vandervord that the pier would be built in a place "Of the best for water and the greater accommodation of the wagons, horses and carters".

The vexed question of tolls and when they were payable was raised but again this was bypassed as the Pier Act precluded the imposition of tolls until the pier had reached 1,500 feet in length. It was also stated that tolls could be levied only when "it would be safe and convenient".

After lunch, was what was described as "A very numerous and respectable meeting of the neighbouring farmers and inhabitants of Southend and Prittlewell". Again, William Heygate was in the chair. He said he understood "That many farmers objected to the proposed measures, but from what he had heard in the room that morning, and from other communications that had been made to him, he had great hopes that the Pier Act would be supported". He also repeated that, "Unless the pier proposal is met with general concurrence, he would abandon it forthwith".

Many shippers of corn attended. They included Messrs Tabor, Stallibrass, Thorn, Silversides and others. Collectively they expressed "Their assent and good wishes to the pier." So, it seems consensus had been achieved and the whole company appeared unanimous—"They wanted only particulars of the dues to be demanded". Heygate, backed by General Strutt and other members of the Pier Company, gave suitable explanations which satisfied the meeting.

A drawing of the pier and jetty was produced for inspection which showed that the pier would give great protection and facility to shipping and craft, as well the farmers' wagons and horses. (see pages 9, 32 and 33). The proposed pier tolls a were then gone through again, item by item, which after some discussion, principally between William Heygate, Mr. Thorn, the corn merchant, and the Vandervords were unanimously agreed. Heygate also stated that, when introduced, the proposed tolls would be fixed low; in fact half the price of what was charged at Margate.

Notable absentees from the meeting were Daniel Scratton and his son. Daniel Scratton was the Lord of The Manor of Milton and owned land needed for pier landside access. The family also had foreshore rights. The Scrattons had already indicated they intended to oppose the Pier Bill on account of the perceived damage the pier and its construction would cause to oyster fisheries. Scratton, through manorial rights exercised by the Southend Oyster Company, laid claim over some 800 acres of foreshore in front of Marine Parade for oyster laying. Whilst he claimed support by fishermen, some of whom had signed a petition in support, this was not necessarily always the case. There had been a series of disputes where some of the Oyster Company's tenants had tried to bar other water users access to the areas they controlled.

Nevertheless, William Heygate and his fellow board members said, "It is their opinion that there would be no injury whatsoever to either Mr. Scratton or the fishermen, but if it should so prove, no doubt the Act would be so framed, as to award them a liberal remuneration".

Just before the meeting broke up, a large body of fishermen arrived from Leigh, "Who, after regaling themselves with some bread, cheese, and ale, expressed to Sir William their hearty good wishes for the pier". This of course contrasted with what Daniel Scatton was reportedly to have said. The fishermen now "Said they were ready to sign a petition to support the Pier Act". Sir William Heygate expressed his gratitude with the reception and that "Unanimity had prevailed".

Following the meeting's conclusion Sir William departed. Outside the Royal Hotel he climbed into his carriage and started off for London, "Amidst the shouts of many and the good wishes of all the inhabitants of Southend."

DELICATE NEGOTIATIONS

Separately, as the pier bill awaited royal assent there was the thorny question of acquiring land for pier access and dealing with the owners of oyster beds and fishing grounds that were a feature of Southend seafront.

The Pier Act stipulated that the pier structures were not to extend westward farther than a direct line drawn from the northernmost extremity of Miller's Hardway to a spot at the low water mark, which was a distance of 1,300 yards from a spot under the cliffs called Mill Gut, nor extend within 800 yards to the southeast of the Mill Gut without the consent of a William Alston, the owner of the shore, or his successors, or the owner "Of a certain a watercourse called the Swatch".

William Alston had humble beginnings. He was born in Prittlewell and started as a butcher and cow keeper. He was nevertheless enterprising and had a sharp business mind. He diversified into oyster fisheries. As business grew, he acquired the Manor of Minster in Sheppey (Kent), as the result of an order of the Court of Chancery. For thirty years right up to the time the Pier Bill received royal assent Alston acquired and consolidated numerous oyster fisheries on both sides of the River Thames. He founded a sales stall at Billingsgate fish market and a coal distribution depot. In addition, he owned some forty sail ships - mainly smacks and hoys, all registered in Rochester. These vessels worked principally in support of William's oyster business - *Alston Oyster Fisheries*.

In 1795 he married Sarah Loader and moved house to Rochester. All the while Alston retained his Essex oyster beds that lay in the shoals around Hadleigh Ray, the narrow channel that runs east to Leigh on Sea and on to Canvey Island.

William Alston's son, David Thomas, (although living in Sheerness) was also involved in early Southend. Daniel Scratton, as mentioned earlier, another Oyster Fishery owner, let two pieces of sea ground (which lay principally between the Mill Gut and the Pier Hardway) to David Thomas Alston.

The process of acquiring land for pier access required delicate negotiations. Prominent people of the town had to be compensated. Daniel Scratton already had some misgivings about the pier project.

Apart from fishery interests, Scratton also owned land that had to be crossed to gain access to the pier. However, Sir William Heygate assured him that he would be compensated for any loss of land and that the pier would not impact on the oyster beds. So, at this stage Daniel Scratton gave his support to the pier project.

The Pier Company also needed support from a Lady Charlotte Denys who lived on Pier Hill in Bow Window House. The Pier Company had promised "No pier, warehouse or building could be erected on the cliff in the possession of Lady Charlotte Denys or within the immediate vicinity of the same without her consent".

The matter was solved when the Pier Company paid £200 to Charotte Denys for land and promised also, "To lay a good and sufficient carriage road from the Royal Hotel down the hill to Lower Southend".

THE FIRST PIER ACT
(also known as the South-end Pier and Improvement Bill)

Much to William Heygate's delight the Pier Act, also known as the *South-end Pier and Improvement Bill*, received Royal Assent on 14th May 1829. The Act, which authorised the pier's construction, included conditions to improve what was Royal Hill, now known as Pier Hill. A new shore road to Shoebury (Clause III) would be built and a more direct route to Prittlewell would be opened (Clause IV). The principal clauses of the bill are shown on page 39.

In 1829, not only was travelling from London to Southend difficult by land or by water, but simply moving around the urban area was a challenge in what today is called greater Southend. For example, people living outside Prittlewell had to travel every Sabbath across fields when they wanted to attend a service at St. Mary's Church, their nearest place of worship.

The original cost of the pier work was estimated at £12,000. This was comprised of £3,685 for piers and jetties including the purchase of land and premises. A further £3,242 was budgeted for the causeway, sluices, and breakwaters and £300 for baths and bathing places. An allowance of £1,569 was put aside for contingencies.

An established Essex bank, *Messrs Sparrow, Tufnell & Co.* was chosen as the principal banker. The bank had been established in 1801 with branches in Bury, Sudbury, and Stowmarket. However, in 1812 Sparrows essentially became an Essex bank of which Mr James Goodeve Sparrow was the senior partner.

An Essex bank Messrs Sparrow, Tufnell & Co five pound note issued in 19th May 1865 (equivalent in 2025 to £775.00)

The principal place of business was Braintree. Over the next 20 years the bank expanded to open branches in Chelmsford, Maldon, Witham and Bishops Stortford. The bank subsequently moved its headquarters to the County town of Chelmsford. In 1896 Sparrow bank was absorbed by Barclay's Bank.

The powers of the new Pier Company extended along the Southend's shoreline to include any goods, wares and merchandise that were landed within three miles of *Ship Tavern* to be carried overland from what was then Lower Southend. This was a vast area, including the parish of Southchurch and part of the parish of Prittlewell and extended from the eastern boundary of the parish of Southchurch to the western boundary of Chalkwell Hall Farm. It should be noted that the Thorpe Hall estate was exempt from pier dues, as were journeys connected with the harvesting of shellfish from the foreshore unless the pier or jetty was then used subsequently to ship shellfish.

The Pier Company had the power to make two piers or jetties with causeways within the limits of the sea beach lying between what was then known as the Lower Southend Road, which led from Prittlewell on the east to what was known then as Wilson's Jetty on the west. Today what we would say would be from the Kursaal to the bottom of Pier Hill.

THE FIRST PIER ACT
ALSO KNOWN AS THE SOUTH-END PIER AND IMPROVEMENT BILL

PRINCIPAL CLAUSES

1-LT IS PROPOSED TO CONSTRUCT A PIER AND JETTY, OR CAUSEWAY, FROM THE SHORE TO THE DEEP WATER, WHERE A FLAG WILL BE HOISTED AND A LIGHT KEPT CONSTANTLY BURNING IN THE NIGHT, SO THAT PASSENGERS, AS WELL AS GOODS, MAY SHIPPED ALL TIMES THE TIDE, WITHOUT THE DELAY, INCONVENIENCE, AND ACCIDENT, WHICH HAVE BEEN SO LONG AND JUSTLY COMPLAINED OF.

11.-A CONVENIENT AND HEALTHY PROMENADE WILL LIKEWISE BE FURNISHED BY MEANS OF THESE WORKS TO THE PUBLIC.

111.-LT IS INTENDED TO CONSTRUCT, REPAIR, AND SECURE CERTAIN ROADS, ESPECIALLY THAT IMPORTANT ONE WHICH CONNECTS UPPER WITH LOWER SOUTHEND, WHICH HAS LONG BEEN IN A DISGRACEFUL STATE OF DECAY AND DANGER, AND FOR THE REPAIR OF WHICH, (AS ORIGINALLY A PRIVATE ROAD,) ALTHOUGH LONG AND UNIVERSALLY USED BY THE NEIGHBOURHOOD, AND ABSOLUTELY NECESSARY FOR THE PUBLIC CONVENIENCE, THERE EXISTS NO FUND WHATEVER. ALSO, TO REPAIR AND CONSTRUCT, WHERE NECESSARY, A ROAD ALONG THE SHORE BY THE SEASIDE, SO AS TO FORM AT ONCE A BEAUTIFUL DRIVE, AND A VALUABLE COMMUNICATION FOR THE PURPOSES OF AGRICULTURE, AND THUS TO OPEN AN IMPORTANT AND FERTILE TRACT OF COUNTRY, NOW ONLY TO BE APPROACHED BY A CIRCUITOUS INTERNAL ROAD.

1V.-LT IS PROPOSED TO OPEN A SHORT AND CONVENIENT COMMUNICATION, LEADING DIRECT TO THE PARISH CHURCH OF PRITTLEWELL, A SPACIOUS AND VENERABLE EDIFICE, AND THE ONLY PLACE OF RELIGIOUS WORSHIP THE ESTABLISHMENT IN THIS POPULOUS AND INCREASING PARISH, IN LIEU OF THE PRESENT COMMUNICATION, WHICH IS CIRCUITOUS AND IN WINTER NEARLY IMPASSABLE: A SERIOUS IMPEDIMENT THE ATTENDANCE OF THE POOR AT THE PARISH CHURCH WILL THUS BE REMOVED AND DIMINISHED.

V.-THE PROPOSED ACT WILL GIVE POWER TO IMPROVE THE PRESENT BATHS AND BATHING-PLACES; AND BY KEEPING PURE THE SPRINGS OF EXCELLENT WATER, AND CLEANSING THE WATER-COURSES, TO ADD TO THE HEALTH AND COMFORT OF THE INHABITANTS.

THE FIRST PIER ACT RECEIVED THE ROYAL ASSENT. 14TH MAY 1829

Yet with all the best laid plans there was a problem. Tolls could not be charged until the pier had been completed to a length of 1,500 feet. Furthermore, the Pier Act specified work must stop if it was not completed within five years. The Pier Company had a dilemma. No tolls meant no income whilst at the same time funds were being eaten up in all directions. Speed in construction of the pier was the order of the day.

CELEBRATION

On Saturday 16th May 1829, following the Pier Act having received Royal Assent two days earlier, a triumphant William Heygate travelled in style down the River Thames from London. He sailed on the yacht, *Sir Joseph York*. As the yacht approached the shore at Southend it was met by a flotilla of small boats. All of the boats were decorated with blue ribbons and one carried a music band.

Heygate stepped down from the *Sir Joseph York* and clambered aboard a waiting boat, described as one the watermen's best, which also carried an awning. The boats then lined up and rowed in an orderly procession to a point opposite the *Ship* tavern (close to the present day Kursaal) before turning west to Miller's Hardway, (see page 9) which served the Royal Hotel. There "A crowd of hundreds of inhabitants, stretching from the foot of the slope to the crest, gave William Heygate a voracious welcome". The ladies of Sir William's family were also waiting on a balcony in Royal Terrace and as soon as Sir William appeared they too began waving greetings with their handkerchiefs.

Crowds had also gathered on Royal Terrace. Sir William soon emerged and took out his handkerchief and waved. He then asked for silence and announced, "I can report the pier has received Royal Assent and we can now finally go ahead and build it". The crowds erupted in cheering and a band struck up. There was great celebration.

An article in the *Essex Herald* heaped praise on Sir William, "We do not wish to give Mr Heygate more credit than is due to him, but we really think he deserves our best praises, when the very great exertions that he has made in carrying this bill through Parliament are considered. Should the works immediately commence (and it is generally thought they will) many a poor fellow who is now destitute of a loaf will perhaps be enabled not only to supply his family with bread, but now and then a pint of beer to drink success to the *South-End Pier Improvement Bill*. It is supposed, should the improvements all go on together, that very a numerous body of workmen will be employed."

Mrs Isabella Heygate, Sir William's wife, had come by carriage to Southend two days earlier and was "Met on the road by crowds who drew the carriage into Southend".

The carriage by now was bedecked with blue ribbons. "Afterwards the crowd regaled themselves with refreshments, at Mrs Heygate's expense".

With a surge in hotels being built in Southend, the need for ship to shore transport was never more paramount. "Owners of properties on Royal Terrace bridged this gap a little by building a jetty opposite the Royal Hotel", and financing the laying of 'hards,' on which horse drawn vans might be driven at low tide to collect passengers and baggage coming ashore from ships.

LAYING THE FOUNDATION STONE

With the Pier Act having received Royal assent and following Sir William's triumphant return to Southend bringing the news, the serious business of building the pier began. However, to keep the momentum going the first steps had to be flamboyant and spectacular.

The *Morning Post* wrote "On 25th July the Lord Mayor of London Sir William Thompson laid the foundation stone of the first section of the pier. This followed his return from holding the Septennial Court as Conservator by ancient charter of the River Thames and Waters of the Medway".

The paper continued, "His Lordship was received amidst the firing of cannon and the cheers of the spectators, and by the authorities of the place". (it was estimated the event was seen by more than 2,000 people.) "The Lord Mayor was attended by the Sheriffs of London and Middlesex, several of the Aldermen of London, Captain Stewart, of his Majesty's ship *Gloucester*, and a great concourse of persons, including many of the Magistrates, Gentry, Clergy, and inhabitants of the neighbourhood and from the county of Kent". There following a speech where the Lord Mayor said "he rejoiced in the opportunity of a public work which promised so much local and general convenience, so closely identified with the trade and commerce of the River Thames and River Medway". He concluded by wishing the project every success.

The mayor's party and invited guests then adjourned to the Royal Hotel for lunch after which the Lord Mayor offered a vote of thanks and returned to London. This was followed in the evening by a gala dinner and speeches. Present were the members of the Southend Pier Company and what might be described as the who's who of Southend and district. During the dinner it was announced that the Lord Bishop of London was due to visit Southend to bless the stone.

In contrast to the extravagant ceremony of laying the foundation stone, a week earlier on 18th July, without fanfare, the first pier timber piles had been driven into the mud, but that event received barely any mention in the press.

THE CONSTRUCTION OF THE FIRST WOODEN PIER

Due to missing records details of the pier's early construction are incomplete. E W Shepherd in his book, *The Story of Southend Pier,* wrote "The Pier Act authorised the construction of a pier, or piers, jetty or jetties, causeway or causeways (not more than two of each category) and of the necessary buildings, such as toll-gates, toll houses, warehouses and a wharf, appurtenant thereto; and also of breakwaters, baths and bathing-places; and of roads, avenues and approaches to the said pier or piers; and authorised the repair, widening and improvement of the road or way leading from the Hadleigh-Southchurch road to Upper Southend, and continuing along the side of the sea-beach in front of Lower Southend, to a house called the Castle Tavern". Shepherd added "In spite of the urgency, only three men were at first directly involved in building the pier; a carpenter, a labourer and an engineer".

At this very early stage General Strutt expressed concern about the pier finances. However, Strutt was assured by other members of the Pier Company that all was in order and "Other employees would be taken on as the work progressed". Yet Shepherd added "The engineer was put on half pay, not out of any disrespect to him, it was stressed, but of necessity. Before long though the engineer's pay was restored and work on the pier continued".

James Walker FRS
1781 –1862

The civil engineer chosen to manage the pier's construction was James Walker, a Scotsman born in Falkirk and a Fellow of the Royal Society (FRS). He was well-known and had a distinguished career. Locally, following his work on the pier, he designed the hexagonal Chapman Lighthouse in Canvey* that stood for over 100 years. He was an associate of Thomas Telford and had gained considerable experience through working on the design and construction of the West India, East India and Surrey docks in London.

Between 1834 and 1845 he was President of the Institution of Civil Engineers and Chief Engineer of Trinity House, a post that required extensive involvement with coastal engineering and lighthouse projects.

To construct the pier from wood a vast amount of timber was needed. Ninety English oaks were used as well as timber imported from Memel and Dantzic. These two ports gave their names to the wood which was shipped from them. Dantzic timber was grown chiefly in Prussia. Dantzic is now called Gdansk, in Poland. This timber was described as strong, tough, elastic, easily worked and durable, if well-seasoned. Memel (now in Lithuania) was a very similar timber to Dantzic, but considered less strong. Its advantage though, was its straight growth, for the small proportion of sap contained within and for its freedom from knots.

The *Morning Advertiser* 29th June 1829 reported that "The COMMITTEE of the SOUTHEND PIER COMPANY hereby give notice, that they will be ready to receive Tenders at my Office. No. 6, New Broad Street, on or before one o clock, on THURSDAY, 2nd July, to supply all or any the following Articles, viz., (at per load) Ninety English Oak Trees, thirty of which to be 24 feet long, and the remaining sixty 30 feet long, all to be 12 inches in diameter, 14 feet from the butt—they must be straight, warranted sound, and as free from sap as possible; also about Sixty Loads of sound Memel or Dantzic Timber, fifty feet long and upwards; also, at per foot run, 5,000 of good sound yellow Memel or Dantzic Plank, three inches by eleven inches, clear of sap. The above Articles be delivered in a fortnight from the acceptance of the Tender, into a barge lying at or near the Grand Surrey Canal Dock, Rotherhithe; or, if more convenient to the parties tendering, on the Shore at Southend, Essex. Signed EDWARD MACKMURDO, Clerk".

Despite Strutt's financial concerns, building work pressed on. The timbers were delivered, more workers hired and within a year the first section of the wooden pier, some six hundred feet long, was opened to the public.

* The Chapman's lighthouse was demolished in 1957–1958 because of its poor condition.

PROGRESS

The Pier Company had also been active on the landside of the pier. In one of a series of letters written by General Strutt on 31st August 1829, about building progress, he wrote,

"Mr. James Heygate (junior) marks out the road over the common," (the common which at that date stretched eastwards along the lower front from Pier Hill to Shoeburyness, lying between the beach and the line of houses fronting it). Strutt added, "Mr. Heygate went as far as the "Poor House" in Southchurch", which the general observed, "Ought certainly to be bought."

On September 18th, the general records "The purchase from Lady Charlotte Denny of Pier Hill and some adjacent ground, for the sum of £200" and on the 21st September he wrote that "The Pier Company has decided upon the site and route of the road to be constructed along the front at lower South End and to purchase and demolish the workhouse at Southchurch". Again, on October 9th he refers to the building of a retaining wall at the shore end of the jetty.

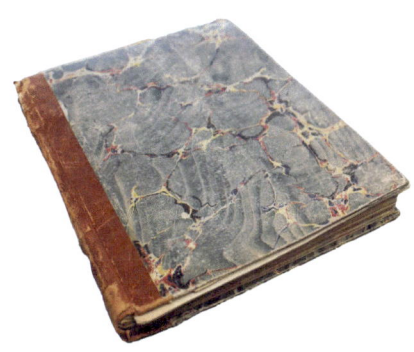

General Strutt's letter-books cover the period from February 11th 1829, until October 9th 1838, a period of nine years and nearly eight months. The books were written in an era before typewriters were available and looked much like school exercise books of the 1930s.

The books were meticulously handwritten. Not only did the books include Strutt's own letters but also, rewritten in Strutt's own hand, copies of the correspondence received from other board members.

One of General Strutts Letter-books

Unfortunately, there is a gap in the correspondence of more than nine months, (October 13th 1833, to June 4th 1834) during which time two important developments in the construction occurred. These developments were "The erection at the seaward end of the pier of a hut on piles surmounted by a light or beacon for the guidance of ships at night". (*the Mount see page 52*).

Also missing is detail of the construction on the eastward side of the pier; the lower platform for the shipping or landing of goods. (see map page 9).

Except for these omissions, the correspondence contains a very detailed account of the erection of the pier and of the extraordinary difficulties and prolonged and determined opposition which was to come.

Extract from General Strutt's letter book

The first annual meeting of the Pier Company was held on May 8th 1830, at the *George and Vulture Tavern*, in London, and was chaired by Sir William Heygate. A report was presented outlining the following,

"The work had proceeded with vigour and success during the latter half of the year 1829 and through the beginning of 1830. The pier twenty feet wide and nearly six hundred feet long had been completed, whilst another two hundred feet on a reduced scale was nearly finished; that the foot of the hill forming a part of the road leading from Upper to Lower Southend, had been walled with stone; that this road with the cliff of which it formed a part, had been drained and fenced; that breakwaters had been constructed; and that an old vessel called the *Clarence* (named after the Duke of Clarence), had been purchased. The *Clarence* was about 100 feet long, fitted up and anchored in the deep water opposite the end of the pier".

The vessel provided accommodation for visitors disembarking from steamboats or other vessels at low tide. It was intended that such persons should first be put aboard the *Clarence* "And from there taken in boats to the pier-head, or, if the tide was at the ebb, to the head of the causeway leading to the pier". The report also stated, "That some boats were being built to carry passengers from the *Clarence* to the shore, thus enabling them to land without danger or inconvenience".

So, by the spring of 1830, good headway had been made with the construction. The builders had also been fortunate that the weather had been kind and that no storms had caused serious damage and delay during the winter months.

The stop-gap landing point for Southend at low tide.
The Clarence moored in deep water.

By 1833 the pier had been extended to a distance of fifteen hundred feet, and a causeway constructed connecting it with deep water, which obviated the need to use vans for landing. The minutes recorded thus,

"An upper platform, fifteen hundred feet in length and twenty feet in width, terminating in an enclosed building called the *Octagon*. From this building the platform continued, but at a narrower width, to the end". By March 1834 "A lower platform for the landing or loading of goods, two hundred and thirty-four feet in length, the greater part constructed of wood but the landward section of stone, had been completed. Also completed was a breakwater enclosing an area on the eastward side of the pier at the shore end. This constituted a harbour for the protection of barges and other vessels making use of the pier. The harbour entrance was forty feet wide".

The pier around 1835 showing the view of the harbour on the east side for loading and unloading barges.

THE OCTAGON

A feature of the new pier was the *Octagon,* a canvas tent structure, covered in and completely protected from the weather, that was sited near the pier head. It was an all-purpose entertainment space, used for refreshments and musical performances. It was a very popular venue and survived until the old wooden pier gave way to the iron structure.

The pier entrance and the tent like structure of the Octagon shown to the right

Again, sadly very little detail has survived about the Octagon. John Burrows, the Essex historian, in his book *Southend Pier and its Story*, quotes two events held in the Octagon,

"The *Octagon* on the Pier was quickly brought into use. It was completely covered, so protected from the weather. It was announced that on October 12th 1831, a public breakfast would take place attended by members of the Pier Company and their guests. A rowing match was advertised to take place after the breakfast, and in the evening there would be dancing at the Royal Hotel, at which the Weippart's Band would attend". The Weippart Band was a popular band of the period, well known on the London musical scene.

Burrows also wrote that a "A fair was held in the Octagon, in 1833, in aid of the fund for building a church in Southend".

SOUTHEND

Published 1875 by the Ordnance Survey Offices
Southampton

Site of original
chain pier

The pier around 1875 showing the view of the harbour on the east side for loading and unloading barges.

THE MOUNT

As noted in the last chapter the *Clarence*, the old ship moored in deep water, was only a stop gap measure. During 1933/4 the ship was replaced by a new structure called the *Mount*, a fixed landing stage constructed on 38 wooden Memel fir timber piles and set in deep water that stood alone and was some 5,000 feet from the so far completed pier head. The *Mount* enabled passengers and their baggage to disembark from ships at all stages of the tide.

Once on the *Mount*, Passengers would then be taken from the *Mount* in small boats to the causeway leading to the pier head. The structure was surmounted by a lantern, and a pharo-light for the guidance of ships. Accommodation was provided for two keepers who had responsibly for maintaining the light. The *Mount* was described by the unkind as "A cluster of piles in the sea". It soon was dubbed 'Mount Misery' as passengers, after landing there, frequently had to endure a muddy walk at low tide to get to the pier head.

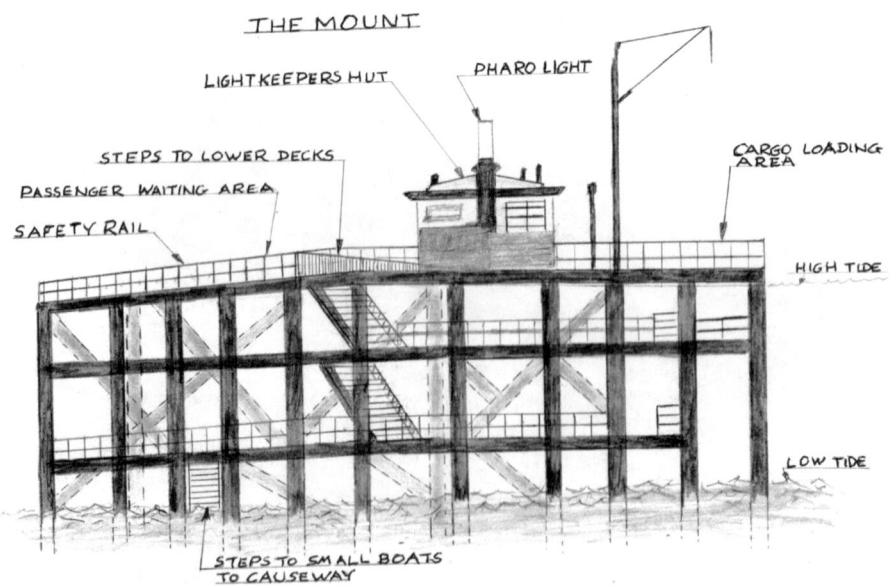

THE MOUNT

LIGHT KEEPERS HUT PHARO LIGHT

STEPS TO LOWER DECKS CARGO LOADING AREA

PASSENGER WAITING AREA

SAFETY RAIL

HIGH TIDE

LOW TIDE

STEPS TO SMALL BOATS TO CAUSEWAY

THE SECOND PIER ACT

The original 1829 Pier Act expired after five years. The Pier Company was therefore obliged to seek the renewal of its legal powers and authority to enable it to extend the pier into deep water. A new Act of Parliament would provide this which became known as the *Southend Pier Amendment Act (1835)*.

In a letter dated May 11th 1835, Sir William Heygate informed Major-General Strutt that the *Southend Pier Amendment Act* had been read a second time in the previous month and that it was to go into committee on the following Wednesday. Heygate added that strong opposition was to be anticipated at that stage from Mr. Scratton, Dr. Nolan (the Vicar of Prittlewell), the Vandervords and others.

James Vandervord opposed Heygate's bill and presented a petition against it. This was debated in the House of Commons. Extracts of the minutes of the meeting are shown in the appendix shown on page 84.

General Strutt, a key member of the Pier Company had bought Rayleigh House on the lower front at Southend, today's Marine Parade. He also owned a sailing boat called the *True Blue*. He was keen to ensure that the views from his house should not be obstructed by the pier or any connected buildings. Accordingly, he seems to have "Gone to endless trouble in his desire for an uninterrupted sea view" and stopped any "Undesirable buildings being built in front of his house", by securing a clause into the proposed Pier Bill when it was being drafted.

General Strutts name still remains by the side of the building formerly known as Rayleigh House in the form of Struts Passage on Southend's Marine Parade. Note the variation on spelling of the name

Despite the opposition the new *Southend Pier Amendment Act* was slowly making its way through parliament. The pier was also now officially on the map!

A copy of a chart of the River Thames surveyed by order of the Lords Commissioners of Admiralty in 1834, by F Bullock, Commander R.N.

A year earlier the Admiralty had created a map of the Thames Estuary showing the pier, the causeway and the *Mount* with a lighthouse.

Also visitors who came to Southend could buy tickets to walk (or promenade) on the pier. At last the pier was generating some income.

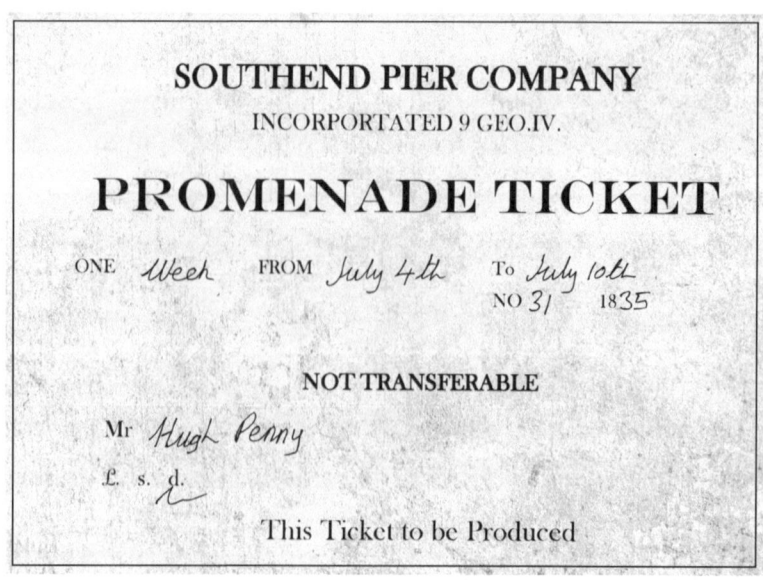

A handwritten pier promenade ticket issued to a Mr Penny in July 1835.

PROBLEMS

To summarise, by 1835, the Southend Pier Company had built a wooden pier from the shore, that started below the Royal Hotel and stretched 1,500 feet into the estuary. At the end of the pier was a covered area known as the *Octagon* that also acted as a hospitality suite. At high tide relatively large vessels could tie up and discharge or load cargo, passengers and their luggage.

The pierhead was the starting point for a 5,000 foot causeway (or hard) that ran to the *Mount,* as described in the previous chapter. The *Mount*, located in deep water was "A hut built of two rooms, inhabited by people deputed to take care of a pharo-light for the safety of vessels at night".

Ships could now tie up day or night no matter what the state of the tide. Passengers then waited on the *Mount* for the tide to recede before taking a boat a short distance to the causeway (that was uncovered at low tide), thereafter making their way along the causeway on foot to the completed section of the pier and then on to the shore.

The *Mount* was advantageous for shipping companies as it enabled vessels to keep better timetables as they were no longer dependant on the state of the tide when dropping off passengers for Southend.

The members of the Pier Company should have been jubilant once this milestone had been reached. Instead, there was deep anxiety expressed especially by General Strutt.

The financial situation was dire. The original cost of the pier work was estimated at £12,000 but to date expenditure of nearly £20,000 had been incurred. Furthermore, the new parliamentary act was needed to complete the pier into deepwater. At the same time many of the original pier supporters were hostile to any more pier work being undertaken and were actively doing all they could to block the passage of the proposed bill through parliament.

Also weighing heavily on the Heygate family was the fact that James Heygate junior had been forced to resign from his bank because of his embezzlement. The shame was soon followed by the death of James Heygate senior.

On practical matters the building of the *Mount* was just another stop gap. Although beneficial to shipping companies the *Mount* only offered rudimentary facilities for passengers coming to Southend. At low water, the travellers had to climb down steps from the *Mount* with their luggage (see page 52). Next, they had to clamber into small boats to take them a short distance to the causeway. Thereafter passengers had to walk with their luggage for at least half a mile to where the so far finished pier began. Even at low tide the causeway had large puddles of standing water and could be covered with seaweed, mud and other detritus the tide had brought in. With rain and a chill wind blowing, it could be quite unpleasant to walk along the causeway. The experience was succinctly put by a Southend shopkeeper. He said "When the steamboat could come alongside the pier, the new structure was a great convenience, but at low water that was definitely not the case before the pier," he added, "We used to ride dry shod for one shilling; now we walk wet for 1s. 6p."

At low tide for a while 'vans' (specially built horse drawn wagons) were sent along the causeway to the *Mount* to collect passengers and baggage, but there were still difficulties. Another tripper said, "There were many problems disembarking from the *Mount* as the van drivers had to be very cautious of high winds and fast running tides."

Sometimes, when passengers were landed at low water on the beach by the *Mount*, they had to sit for hours in all weathers waiting for the vans to fetch them. There were two vans, one operating from the Ship Inn, and the other from the Royal Hotel. It was reported that as many as two hundred people had been landed on Saturday afternoons.

There were also issues with ships docking at the so far finished pier, even at high tide. Captain Joseph Wallace of the 126 ft long *William IV* explained that his steamboat (which had run daily to and from Southend since 1829) had difficulty making fast on the pier head as it was 70ft shorter than the vessel. This necessitated "Making use of a rough tree rail that was liable to be pulled up if there was a swell".

Other ship's captains were also wary about approaching the pier head (as opposed to the *Mount*) for if the tide was running fast and there was a delay in passenger disembarkation or embarkation the vessel could become stranded as the water receded.

Just to add to all the practical issues another objection came from fisherman. They complained that the wall protecting the causeway (only a couple of feet high) constituted a hazard to fishing boats when the water was low and the "Lighthouse on the *Mount* was a danger to navigation as the ebb tide set it on and the flood tide turned it off". Leigh fishermen dubbed the structure *"Mount Misery"*. At the time the Leigh fishing fleet consisted of nearly 170 vessels. *Mount Misery* also seemed an apt description for passengers stuck there waiting to get to shore.

OUTRIGHT OPPOSITION

The Heygates and the Southend Pier Company were being buffeted from all sides.

The most vociferous opposition came from the Vandervord shipping family. Running a shipping business, without the benefit of modern navigational aids and communication, in the age of sail in a fast tidal area such as the Thames Estuary was a challenge at the best of times. Winter storms and tides could strand vessels for days or even weeks at a time.

However, the Vandervord family were used to overcoming setbacks. In 1827 "William Heard Vandervord, George John Vandervord and James Wilson Vandervord, described as hoymen, corn and coal merchants" were collectively declared bankrupt. Despite this they managed to refinance the business and keep going.

In their opposition to the pier the Vandervords were supported by the Scrattons, many fishermen, watermen and farmers. The Vandervords were seething as they were under the impression that Sir Willliam Heygate had promised to build a second loading pier east of the (new) pier, where the Kursaal is now sited. William Heygate in no uncertain terms denied that he had ever made that promise.

The Vandervords were also extremely dissatisfied with what had been built so far. The pier was made of wood and not stone. "To call this wooden contrivance a pier is quite farcical. It is too high above the water for landing or shipping goods".

Apparently only five barges had used the 'harbour' during the five years it had existed. The harbour also contained decayed seaweed that caused a bad smell which was noticeable even on Royal Terrace.

A period sailing barge, possibly the Minerva, one of the Vandervord vessels (see also appendix page 87)

SOUTHEND
PIER COMPANY.

Messrs. VANDERVORDS, beg leave to inform the Public, that the *Five Years granted by the Legislature to the above Company, for the Completion of their Works having expired on Friday, July 31st*, and as by Clause 15 of the last Act they were bound to carry their Jetty down to low Water Mark, under the Penalty of the forfeiture of their Dues for non-compliance with the same, but so far from having done so, they have not had the Inclination or Ability to carry it one inch further, it is under such circumstances, the Act declares in the said Clause, that the Tolls as far as "Agricultural Produce, Goods, Wares, and Merchandize are concerned, shall cease and determine."

The Company, however, unable to complete their Works, are still more reluctant to release their hold on the Public Purse, and as a last resource, (drowning Men (*query* Rats) will catch at straws) have published a hand Bill stating that the said Clause is of non-effect, in opposition to which, and that the Public may have a clear knowledge of the matter, we beg to lay before them the copy of an opinion of *Sergeant Ludlow's* taken in November last, not by ourselves, but by a Gentleman of this Neighbourhood as follows : ---

Copy of Opinion upon the 15th Clause of the Southend

AMENDMENT ACT.

By the 91st Section of the Original Act, 10 Geo. 4. cap. 49. certain goods landed within certain limits were made liable to the payment of the duties chargeable under the Act, but it does not appear to me that under this or under any other Provision, which I can find either in that Act, or the Act of the 5 & 6 Wm. 4. cap. 90., the operation of the 15th Section of the latter Act is qualified or affected, in the event therefore, which is anticipated that the works mentioned in that 15th Section, should not be completed in the five years from the passing of that Act, I think that the Rates and Duties, authorized to be taken by the former Act, in respect of Goods, Merchandize, and Agricultural produce, **CANNOT** after the expiration of that Five Years be required to be paid, unless the parties shall use the works of the Company, and it does not appear to me that this non-liabillity, will be affected by the Assignment to the Commissioners of Exchequer Bills, mentioned in the 12th Section of the latter Act.

Signed, **EBENEZER LUDLOW,**
Sergeants Inn, 29th November, 1839.

We lay this before the Public, without Note or Comment, simply stating, that in conformity with this opinion, we shall load at Southend every Saturday as usual, and conduct our Business in the same manner as before the Decision came to at the CHELMSFORD QUARTER SESSIONS, in JANUARY, 1839.

J. PAPINEAU, PRINTER, 19, MARK LANE.

A poster commissioned by the Vandervords highlighting their dissatisfaction with the pier.

The Vandervords repeated the fishermen's complaints about the causeway wall, the concerns of Captain Joseph Wallace of the *William IV* and the inconvenience and discomfort for passengers making their way from the *Mount* at low tide. James Vandervord summed up by saying "The situation was more inconvenient and uncomfortable now in 1835 than it was before the erection of the pier".

In a letter of August 12th 1835, Major-General Strutt informed James Heygate junior of this opposition.

"The Vandervords, the residents and the farmers have formed a committee to petition parliament (appendix page 84) opposing the new pier act. They were supported by Daniel Scratton who had donated £50.00 towards the expenses of the committee. The petition had quickly secured three hundred subscribers". Many Southend residents added their weight to the opposition especially with regard to the imposition of tolls for using the turnpike road leading to the pier.

Tolls authorised by the act of 1829 were vital for financing the pier's extension and without revenue the Pier Company's debts would climb. A prolonged and bitter struggle ensued and is covered at length in Major-General Strutt's correspondence.

The feelings of the townspeople were running high and in General Strutt's words "The present situation in Southend is caused by the contention about the tolls of the turnpike keeping the place in hot water."

The Toll House shown on the left at the entrance to the pier around 1834

Just to recap, the Pier Act of 1829 allowed the Southend Pier Company to levy tolls, once the pier had reached a length of 1,500ft and was functioning in a "fit state". December 1833 saw the erection of a toll booth at the entrance of the pier to facilitate the collection of tolls for cargos landed at Southend. A toll gate was also erected on Pier Hill for using the road between Upper and Lower Southend.

Certain parties were exempted from the tolls. The Lord of the manor of Milton Hall was allowed to attend his oyster laying without being liable to charge, and owners and occupiers of the Thorpe Hall Estate were permitted to ship agricultural produce at their landing places situated at the end of the private road leading from Thorpe Hall through the Great Strand field to the seashore.

The *Essex Herald* of 5th August 1834, reminded its readers that commercial tolls were payable in the area of the Pier Company's jurisdiction.

"The Public are respectfully informed that the Pier in South-End, in the county of Essex, for Landing and Shipping Agricultural Produce, and Goods, and Merchandise, having been made fit for use, the several

Rates or Duties, authorised by the Act of Parliament for building the same, will be collected and taken, from and after the 2nd day of August, for and on account of all such Articles and Things liable thereto, as shall be laden or unladen within the limits specified in the said Act."

Yet, the Vandervords had declared the pier as "Useless", and certainly not fit for use. In so much, they said their shipping business was worst served than before the pier was built. In their opinion although the pier was 1500 feet long, it was not "Functioning in good order".

Grievance with tolls came to a head on Saturday 9th of August 1834, when the barge *Minerva*, of which James Vandervord was Master, decided to ship a quantity of corn and seeds at Lower Southend within the Pier Company's limits, although not at the pier.

Two toll collectors, John Patterson and John Ingram, went to board the *Minerva* to collect the pier dues. However, payment was refused by Vandervord.

The incident was reported as "Mr Ingram put his foot upon the anchor of the barge, with a view to executing distraint. The collectors then attempted to distrain. In their action, both Ingram and Patterson were assaulted by Vandervord who threatened to first to shoot and then throw them overboard. The collectors were compelled to retire". The *Minerva* sailed that night without paying the dues.

Another serious incident took place on land as noted by the *Essex and Herts Mercury of 16th September 1834*, under the headline,

Forcible Removal of the Toll, Southend

"There was a lot of anger. Messrs Vandevord and their men, proceeded with two horses, a hatchet and a chain, to forcibly remove the toll bar. A very serious dispute had arisen between the inhabitants of Southend and the Pier Company". The company considered they had made sufficient improvement in the road to entitle them to collect tolls, and as noted above they had erected a gate about midway down the (Pier) hill. "A toll was demanded of every horse and carriage".

"Vandervord argued the works were incomplete; therefore, the company had no legal claim. On that same Monday morning several of the inhabitants helped the Vandervords.

They first chopped down the bar, then pulled up the posts, and finally threw down the toll-table. The Pier Company threatened to institute proceedings and there the matter rests."

Yet, an extraordinary feature of this struggle was the attitude taken by the local magistrates, who initially refused to convict persons brought before them for non-payment of dues, or for resisting the Pier Company's officers when they attempted to distrain for such non-payment. This was despite the fact that the Pier Act of 1929 clearly gave the company the right of exacting these dues.

In another incident of which the date is unclear, it was reported, "Thirty men assembled to aid James Vandervord. They came armed with handspikes." (Handspikes were a bar or lever, generally of wood, used in a windlass or capstan, for heaving the anchor in a boat. Sometimes the spikes were metal tipped). "The men then proceeded towards the toll bar, which had now been erected for the third time. The posts had been strengthened and cased with iron, but still the men attacked and destroyed them. A magistrate was called out, but he refused to attend."

Apparently, the magistrate had doubts about the interpretation of the Pier Act. The 1929 Pier Act stipulated dues could not be levied until the Pier was complete and in a "Fit state" and in the minds of the Vandervords the pier was "Not fit for purpose".

The whole situation seemed to be getting ever more complex and confusing. In October 1835 it was reported that some watermen refused to pay their pier tolls. Subsequently at Rochford Magistrates Court, the watermen were fined one shilling each for not obeying regulations but whether the fines were paid is not clear.

Much of General Strutt's third volume of letters from June 4th 1834 is taken up with the efforts of the Pier Company to secure the enforcement by the local magistrates of the powers and rights conferred upon it by the parliamentary act of 1929. Strutt's letter emphasised,

"The Company's claims for dues were resisted with violence, its officers assaulted, its toll-gate smashed to pieces, its right to monopoly of the landing or loading of goods within a three miles radius of the *Ship Inn* ignored, and its attempts to obtain a conviction of the offenders in the local Magistrates' courts was constantly thwarted".

In another letter, of August 13th, the general affirmed that "Even the Donkey Boys brave us, saying that we have no Act of Parliament and that they will do as they please."

Sir William Heygate, who was a lawyer by training, was quoted as saying, "The story of the difficulties encountered by the company in securing the enforcement of an Act of Parliament is extraordinary and without parallel in English legal history".

The case of enforcement of pier tolls became an epic struggle between Sir William Heygate's Southend Pier Company and the Vandervord family. Meanwhile the Pier Improvement Bill continued its slow progress through parliament.

In a letter dated June 11th 1835, Mr. James Heygate junior informed General Strutt that the bill had passed the Committee Stage despite strong opposition from the Vandervords who, he wrote, "Had been violent and abusive of everybody in any way connected with the Company."

He asserted that the bill had undergone only one important change in committee, namely the insertion of a clause requiring the extension of the pier to the lighthouse within a period of five years from the passing of the act.

He added that the bill contained no provision for the building of a pier for goods at Lower Southend, which no doubt explains the continuing rage of the Vandervords. The letter ended by stating that "The Company's Collector, John Patterson, had been assaulted and injured by the boatmen at Southend".

From General Strutt's correspondence, a letter of July 6th 1835 tells of Mr. James Heygate junior referring to the progress of the bill in the House of Lords. He said "The opposition are putting up a strenuous fight against it and spending much money in opposing it". In another letter, of July 23rd Heygate informs General Strutt "The Bill's passage through Parliament is assured", Heygate added that, "The opposition had fought the bill inch by inch, and that he had never heard of an opposition to a bill so obstinate and blindly violent".

The bill finally received the royal assent sometime between July 23rd and August 17th 1835, as a letter of the latter date refers to its having been given.

Also in this letter General Strutt refers to the "Intolerable" behaviour of the Southend watermen, whom he declares to be "Masters of the situation". Strutt goes on to affirm his suspicion that the Southend Pier Company is bankrupt.

However, despite the grave financial situation facing the Pier Company as recorded by the General, it seems the struggle with the Vandervords was moving in William Heygate's favour. The reasons were twofold; influence and money.

Firstly, the Pier Company had considerable parliamentary influence. The company members and shareholders (Appendix page 83) included four baronets and two members of parliament who would have been well placed to push the new parliament act though and overcome obstacles put in its way. As far as is known neither the Vandervords nor the Scrattons could rely on anyone in parliament to lobby for them.

On the question of money, the Heygates were exceedingly wealthy in their own right and furthermore once the new *Southend Pier Amendment Act* became law it empowered the company to raise an additional sum of twenty thousand pounds. On the other hand, the Vandervords' finances were stretched. They had been bankrupted once. Apart from the challenges of running a shipping business the Vandervords' principals were continually absent because of their having to spend lengthy periods engaged in court proceedings.

Even what appeared to be the simple matter of raising a petition opposing the new pier bill in parliament was costly. Although it is not known how much it cost to present the petition (estimated at several thousands of pounds) the effort was nevertheless unsuccessful which meant all the costs fell on the petitioners.

The *Chelmsford Chronicle* of 3rd June 1836 gave this account of a hearing that took place at the King's Head Inn, Rochford.

"Pursuant to public announcement a numerous meeting of persons who signed the petition in opposition to the Southend Pier Company, and in consequence of which legal proceedings were taken against the Company by Messrs. Griffith and Son, solicitors, at a cost of several thousands of pounds, a balance of £1,700, it appeared, remained due to the solicitors for costs. So Messrs. Griffiths instituted proceedings against Mr. Scratton, who was a leading petitioner".

The Vandervords were also incurring mounting legal bills from the multiple legal actions brought against them by the Pier Company for non-payment of tolls and associated vandalism.

In 1833 the wooden pier was 1,500 long with the intention to extend the pier into deep water a mile further out.

However, just as the legal disputes were being resolved in the Pier Company's favour a serious problem was evident on the pier itself.

TEREDO NAVALIS
Commonly known as the Naval Shipworm.
Shipworms are highly modified bivalves,
adapted for boring into wood

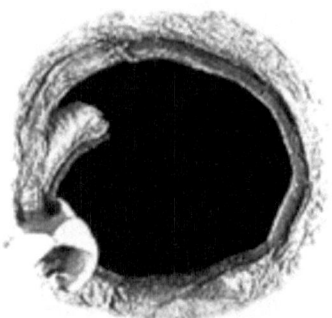

Whilst most of the Pier Company's attention had been focused on legal matters and resolving the tolling issues, there was now a pressing issue building up on the wooden pier itself which had the potential to scupper the whole project.

By 1833 Southend Pier was 1,500 feet long. The original intention was to extend the pier into deep water a mile further out. However, due to circumstances unforeseen or simply ignored no further extension work could be done until much of the existing pier was taken down.

Evidently the wooden pier had been struck by an attack of a species of saltwater clam called *Teredo Navalis*, more commonly called naval shipworm or turu. The turu bores into timber, forming a shell as it progresses.

Such worms can grow to three feet in length with a diameter of up to an inch. The shape of the two shells, forming the extremity of the *Teredo*, admirably adapted them for powerful cutting or rasping tools when they move rapidly in a circular direction This was evident from the uniformly cylindrical character of the holes seen in the pier timbers. A surveyor's report gave the following description.

"The early state of the *Teredo* was noticed; when escaping from the egg, in the shape of a free swimmer, it drifted about with the tide until it met with a log, a pile, or the side of a ship, to which it attached itself, and making an inroad into it became a non-locomotive animal of different form and habits, never again to leave the habitation it had burrowed for itself in the body of the timber".

That this was a big problem was an understatement as such damage was not covered by insurance. In less than four years, the worms had burrowed themselves deep into the timbers to such an extent that some of the piles were entirely eaten through, both above and below the copper sheathing.

Much of the detail of the damage to the pier given below was revealed over 15 years later in the *Minutes of the Proceedings of the Institution of Civil Engineers* in 1850 which recorded,

"The old pier-head consisted of thirty-eight fir-timber piles, driven to a depth of 8 to 10 feet into sand and clay. The upper platform was constructed of fir-timber planking and iron railings and was set about 25 feet above the low water level. The original wood was good quality", as outlined on page 44.

The minutes add, "All the timber work had been well coated with pitch and tar. The pier-head was additionally protected by copper sheathing and had regular brushing and cleaning". Yet, despite the apparent constant monitoring, the ship worm managed to take hold and spread quickly. Without quick and decisive action, the pier would soon become unsafe and its destruction was a real possibility.

The *Teredo Navalis* first showed itself six months after the completion of the work in 1830. Within another twelve months the minutes added "(the worm) to have seriously injured the piles above the copper, whilst at the low-water mark of neap tides, nearly all the piles exhibited appearances of destruction". Just to add to the woes, another wood-boring marine isopod *Limnoria Lignorum,* commonly known as gribble, had joined the *Teredo* in eating the pier away.

"As a consequence of this, the stability of the structure was materially injured, and, on examination, it was discovered that the ground had been considerably washed away by the action of the sea and that the piles, below the copper sheathing, were also exposed to the action of the *Teredo".* The paper also added "As a necessary security to the structure, it was found requisite to drive six new piles: one at each end, and four in the middle, and also to fix some longitudinal timbers on the sides, extending the whole length of the pier. Of course, this was but a temporary security. Heavy seas tore away some of the fixing straps and bolts and pushed the piles out of the perpendicular. It remained in this state for three years, displaying, after every gale of wind, new signs of destruction, until it was considered unsafe, and the men, who until this period had resided in the lighthouse, abandoned it to its fate"*.

As time passed not one of the thirty-eight original fir timber piles, or of the additional oak piles, remained perfect. The majority had been almost destroyed in three years, and by 1844 in addition to the piles being eaten through by the worm, the whole structure had sunk about 9 inches at the western end, so that in a short time it would have fallen.

There seemed no other solution other than to take the existing wooden pier down and start again.

Although the exact date is not known the 'Mount' and its (pharo-light) navigation lights as described on page 52 was abandoned by its resident keepers sometime around 1842 due to the severe deterioration of the structure.

GENERAL STRUTT'S DOUBTS

Major-General William Goodday Strutt was a key member and one of the founders of the Southend Pier Company. Yet, as the pier project progressed Strutt found his role in the company troubling.

As mentioned on page 26 Goodday was the second son of John Strutt of Terling Place, Essex, the home of successive Lords of Rayleigh. His father and brother had had long parliamentary careers. The Maldon constituency was represented by a Strutt for nearly 40 years. Goodday Strutt never stood for parliament but his outlook may well have been influenced by the views of the Strutt's family inside and outside of parliament. Both were anti-slavery and both were concerned about rural poverty.

The general had been a military man who meticulously planned his actions and was used to getting things done. Thus, for him to join a company board comprised of lawyers, city men and three Heygates, who were essentially bankers and large landowners, General Strutt must have felt on his own; outnumbered.

As early as 1932 the general was frustrated with the pier's progress and more pertinently at the way he perceived the other members of the committee were treating him. In a letter of July 19th that year he complained of being treated as a "Mere cypher". He further added that important decisions concerning the undertaking had been made without consulting him and that he had not been kept informed about progress.

He even tendered his resignation. However, he was persuaded by the Heygates to remain, and Sir William expressed the hope that he would not "Desert the undertaking now that we are on the eve of better prospects". The resignation was withdrawn and a year later on May 28th 1833, the Secretary of the Committee informed the general that he had been re-elected to the Committee of Management.

Yet, as the project continued Strutt became more unsettled. In the back of his mind was the Heygates' early dealing with the Vandervords and William Heygate's promise (although later denied) of building a second pier or jetty at the Kursaal site.

This additional pier was later ruled out with the passing of the *1835 Southend Pier Amendment Act* which was another reason why the Vandervords had vigorously petitioned against the act.

Of course, the Vandervords had not helped their case due to their persistent personal attacks on all members of the Pier Company, together with the violence and vandalism that featured in their actions. In the meantime, while not showing it the general "Nursed his wrath" quietly.

The Pier Company's finances continued to be of concern to Strutt. He had brought these to the attention of the company within a year of building work first starting; but his worries were ignored. As time progressed matters did not improve, especially because of the widespread resistance to the paying of any tolls and the discovery of *Teredo Navalis* in the pier timbers. Although not recorded, General Strutt was no doubt also on the receiving end of angry complaints from contractors and suppliers because of delayed or late payments.

The issue of non-payment of tolls loomed increasingly large on the general's mind. This followed another incident on August 12th 1834 when the toll collector, John Patterson, reported that, together with his assistant John Ingram, on boarding George Vandervord's barge the *Royal Oak* to demand payment of pier dues they were threatened with violence if they took anything. In a letter of August 21st Strutt reported the case as coming to court at Rochford, however the magistrate dismissed it.

Strutt was infuriated, especially as Southend Pier Company collectors had again been threatened with violence. The incident prompted Strutt to send a letter to James Heygate stating his intention to prosecute the master of a coal sloop for obstruction, assault and non-payment of dues. In Strutt's eyes, what made matters worse was that the master of the sloop "Had been bragging in the public room of the Ship Inn, that this was his third trip without payment of dues".

The Heygates, however, were opposed to Strutt's proposal and indicated that they were doubtful of securing a conviction. This enraged the general who was greatly offended at being overruled. There followed just over two months silence from the Heygates. Then suddenly in November General Strutt received a letter from William Heygate stating it was now the intention of the company to proceed to prosecute a case

"As soon as one occurred which offered a good chance of securing a conviction."

The general's wrath boiled over. He complained that he had received a "Personal affront" and again tendered his resignation, but the offer was again quietly ignored by the Committee of Management.

Although Royal assent had been given to the new pier bill with provision for acquiring more funds for future work, in a letter of the 17th August 1835 Strutt reiterated his belief that the Southend Pier Company was for all intents and purposes bankrupt, but again this was passed over by the Heygates.

There followed a gap of nearly eighteen months in the general's letters. In later correspondence of both January and May 1837 Strutt urged the erection of a pier for goods at Lower Southend as a means of placating opposition and obtaining a much-needed addition to the company's income. He "Strongly urged its adoption as the most promising, and indeed the only method of rescuing the company from insolvency".

Once again, he was rebuffed by the committee and on September 7th 1837, for the third time, Strutt expressed his wish to resign, alleging that "His opinions concerning the proceedings of the company differed widely from those of other members". Strutt also expressed strong objection to the recent appointment of Elizabeth Anne Heygate (the sister of James and Sir William Heygate) as a member of the committee. He said that this would again raise the representation of the Heygate family to three out of a total of nine, although there is suspicion the objection came because Elizabeth was not a man!

The committee, again, took no notice of the resignation threat hoping, no doubt, that the storm would blow over.

GENERAL STRUTT RESIGNS

With the passing of the Pier Act of 1835 there seemed at last to be a real possibility for the Southend Pier Company to collect its pier tolls. On the 15th October 1935, James Heygate junior informed Major-General Strutt that "At last" the magistrates at Rochford had "Put the Act in force."

Yet, there was still confusion. Other local magistrates continued to show reluctance to enforce the act. Enforcement took years to be finally resolved but by June 1938 General Strutt had had enough.

In a letter of June 3rd 1838, Strutt wrote to Edward Mackmurdo, the Secretary of the Committee of Management, telling him that he was going to resign. This was Strutt's fourth request. He reiterated his earlier complaints saying that they (the committee) had "Declined to act", when he had asked on several occasions and that in his view, he "Had been badly treated". Furthermore "My advice was repeatedly ignored and my opinions regarding the management of the undertaking disregarded." He added, "I was also prevented by my advanced age and infirmities from attending the meetings in London, and thus debarred from expressing my views, which were often at variance with those of colleagues on important questions of policy decided there". He therefore insisted upon resigning this time.

Although the General was embroiled in Pier Company matters, he had also been actively supporting the building of a new Episcopal Chapel or Church in Southend on land just above the pier site. As was mentioned on page 37 the main church for Southend was St. Mary's Church in Prittlewell and people living in Southend or Lower Southend had to trek across fields if they wanted to attend a service there.

Yet, the long-time vicar of St Mary's, Dr Fredrick Nolan, was strongly opposed to this new place of worship, as Southend was part Prittlewell and therefore under Nolan's charge. Nolan argued that St Mary's in Prittlewell could easily cope with the growing population and visitors coming to Southend. Nolan even went so far as to physically prevent the Bishop of London from laying the foundation stone at the new chapel when he came to Southend.

Nolan had a reputation for being stubborn and difficult to deal with. He was not popular in many quarters. He now had General Strutt to contend with. General Strutt was the prime mover of getting the new church and was a member of the Chapel Committee. According to the *Chelmsford Chronicle* "The committee had a number of influential residents".

The general was determined to get the new church built and was supported by his family (Lord Rayleigh). Strutt furnished the new chapel with financial contributions and generous gifts.

Included were "A very handsome communion table, made from a cedar grown in his park, together with a beautifully designed and costly service communion plate".

The Hon. Miss Emily Strutt, the sister of Lord Rayleigh, made "Splendid alter cloths" which were also given to the chapel.

Due in large part to the persistence of General Strutt, Dr Nolan eventually lost out. In 1842, Southend was separated ecclesiastically from Prittlewell and the Church of St John the Baptist (the chapel) came into being. Today St John's Church is sited beside the Park Inn, Palace Hotel.

Meanwhile despite the distractions of the new chapel, pier tolls still loomed large in General Strutt's mind.

In August 1838 another prosecution was dismissed against boatmen who evaded payment of pier dues for landing baggage on the beach in the Pier Company's area of jurisdiction. Yet, although full recognition by the local magistrates of the company's claims still seemed some way off, the Pier Company did have notable success when, also in August 1838, James Heygate junior informed General Strutt that, after a hard-fought case in the Magistrates' Court at Wickford, the company had succeeded in securing the conviction of their principal nemesis the Vandervords for non-payment of dues. George John and James Wilson Vandervord were fined twenty pounds each and William Heard Vandervord five pounds. (see also appendix page 104)

The significance of the judgements was reported at length in both the *Essex Herald* and the *Chelmsford Chronicle*.

"At long last the Pier Company had secured the recognition by the local magistrates of its legal claims to the payment of dues and tolls for the use of the pier and of the approaches to it".

Sir William Heygate said with great satisfaction, that "The prospects of the company were brightening, and that he believed that with firmness, perseverance and exertion, the concern could be brought round."

The Pier Company Committee also then decided to accept the resignation of General Strutt which had been pending since June. On 9th October 1838, Edward Mackmurdo, the Secretary to the Committee, wrote to the general and informed him that his resignation had been accepted and his name "Withdrawn from the direction." The letter contained no word of thanks or appreciation for the General's services!

This curt and ungracious letter ended the correspondence in Strutt's letter-books first mentioned on page 26, and presumably also Major-General Strutt's active work on behalf of the Southend Pier Company

To a certain extent it seems a mystery as to why it took four resignation attempts on the part of the general before it was begrudgingly accepted by the Pier Company. The general was not a member of parliament or the House of Lords although successive members of his family were. Perhaps it was simply that the general had influence in the parts needed that others could not reach!

So ends the history of the Old Southend Pier as far as revealed in General Strutt's letter-books. It is the story of a great enterprise carried on for nine years in the teeth of bitter and persistent opposition. Great credit is due to the men who in such circumstances carried out a project which has been of such advantage to Southend. Among the chief of those to whom credit is due is, surely, is the old soldier, General William Goodday Strutt, who sacrificed a considerable portion of his well-earned period of retirement to the task of supervising the work of construction during nine trying and difficult years.

The short wooden pier in about 1840

INTO DEEP WATER

Despite the Pier Company's success in the courts, apart from superficial improvements, there had been no significant progress on extending the pier into deep water for six years. The discovery of *Teredo Navalis* (the shipworm, see page 66) in the wooden timbers had required time consuming and expensive remedial work and together with a lack of funds and the weeks tied up in court cases, all major works had been delayed.

Perhaps the best description of the pier at the end of the 1830s appeared in Dr Augustus Bozzi Granville's 1841 book, *Spas of England and principal Sea Bathing Places*.

"The wooden jetty at present in existence and the only convenient place people have to land upon extends only to about half a mile and is always left dry at low tides. It is followed out by a line of shingle, projecting perhaps a quarter of a mile farther, and called the Hard. Then follows a space of clear water, even at low tide, which divides the termination of the Hard and a cluster of piles in the sea called the *Mount*, on which a hut is built with two rooms, inhabited by people deputed to take care of a pharo-light for the safety of vessels at night. To this *Mount*, when it is low water, the Gravesend and Southend steamers land their passengers in the summer, who are then boated over to the Hard and thence walk to the jetty. At high water when the weather is not boisterous the steamers land their passengers at the jetty itself. The question of the extension of the latter has suffered various clashing interests for the last ten years, and there is as little probability as ever that desired continuation will ever be accomplished." Despite Dr Augustus Bozzi Granville's doubts about the completion of the pier to deep water he added, "As for the land journey, even with the advantage of rail conveyance as far as Brentwood, the onward journey to Southend is fatiguing and inconvenient compared with the facility and rapidity of a down course by steamers on the Thames. To expect people to come in great numbers by that way (by rail then overland) is absurd."

The *Southend Pier Amendment Act* of 1835 had empowered the company to raise an additional sum of twenty thousand pounds for the financing of the undertaking. How much of this was spent on sorting out the existing pier issues is not known, but another advance was made in 1843 to complete the pier.

Extending the pier to deep water was a massive and complex task, that posed many engineering challenges and where at the same time everything had to be accounted for.

An announcement appeared in *The Surveyor, Engineer and Architect, Vol 4 Issue 47*, of January 1843 showing the vast work and detail involved.

Headed "SOUTHEND Pier. — Government has, we are informed, advanced money for the completion of Southend Pier, and the work has been placed under the management of Mr. Simpson, who is now preparing the drawings and making arrangements for the immediate performance of the work. The works in this specification comprise all the labour, tools, implements, materials, carriages and other things requisite to remove the piles, platform, stairs, and other works in the present pier head and lighthouse platform, and to construct and complete the new pier head and extension of the present pier, including platforms, resting-places, landing-places, and stairs in connection there-with, as shown in the drawings above enumerated. The present lighthouse is to be carefully removed, with a view to its re-erection on the new pier head. This time the pier will be constructed partly with cast-iron piles and partly with timber piles, to which the platforms, resting-places, landing-places, and stairs are to be fixed." (See page 98 appendix for full specification)

The new extension would allow the landing from steamers at low water. James Simpson V.P. Inst. C.E. was a waterworks and manufacturing engineer who had been extensively engaged on various large engineering works in different parts of the country. In 1823 Simpson was the chief engineer to both the Chelsea and Lambeth waterworks companies. In 1825, he became a member of the Institution of Civil Engineers and also in 1825 he went into partnership with George Thompson, an engine maker.

Work on the pier extension began in 1844 and took two years to complete. The new work was nearly a mile long making the whole structure a mile and a quarter (2133m). It was now the longest pier in Europe. The contract was carried out according to the designs of James Simpson by Jonathon Hall, whose company had been involved in the construction of several large railway projects

END OF AN ERA

1843 and 1844 were notable years in the early pier's history though. In July 1843 the principal opponent of the pier, George John Vandervord, then aged 51, passed away and a year later in August 1844 Sir William Heygate (Mr Pier) aged 62, died in London.

Heygate was serving as the Chamberlain of the City of London, a position he had held since the previous year. He was laid to rest in St Margaret's Churchyard, Leicester. Thus, Sir William never got to see the pier extended.

The other significant opponent of the pier was Daniel Robert Scratton, the Lord of the Manor of Milton. His objections to the pier centred around tolls and oyster beds. However, the Southend oyster beds were being contaminated by the discharge of raw sewage released straight into the sea from both Southend and Leigh-on-Sea. Eating contaminated oysters contributed to serious localised outbreaks of typhoid. The resultant heath scares severely damaged sales for Southend's oyster business in London, the principal market.

In 1842 Daniel Robert Scratton inherited the remains of Prittlewell Priory. Together with his wife, Maria, he renovated the buildings to provide a comfortable home. Around this time Scratton seemed to have lost interest in Southend Pier but whether this was because of the problems with oysters, renovating Prittlewell Priory or some other reason is not known. In any event Daniel Scratton later left Southend and moved to Devon.

SOUTHEND PIER COMPLETED

The news of the completion of the pier extension was greeted with joy. Both the *Chelmsford Chronicle* of 29th May 1846 and the *Essex Standard* of 5th June 1846 ran the same report under the above headline. The papers quoted the words of Mr Henry Choules, the manager of the Royal Hotel between 1839 and 1856,

"I have great pleasure in informing my friends and the public that the completion of the Pier, at Southend, enables parties to land or embark at all times of the tide; and I trust that the difficulty of access by water being now removed, Southend will take that rank among the favoured watering-places which, from its delightful situation and the rural beauties of the environs, it so well deserves".

Mr Choules gave thanks to those kind friends whose patronage he had experienced for nearly 12 years. He also assured them of his determination to supply every article of the best quality, and on moderate terms, and to give prompt attention to clients' wishes to promote their comfort and secure their approval.

In the first six weeks of the new pier being open the gross receipts were £160 16s. 1d., that would be £26 a week and estimated at £1,315 a year. Furthermore, the 1s. 6d charge for passengers had been reduced to only 6d which in turn served to boost the numbers landing.

Also, it was considered that when the railway was completed there would be additional revenue of £2,000 to £3,000 a year from tolls, for passengers landing and for promenading. In addition to this, there were the tolls, rates and dues from vessels, which it was calculated would amount to £800. Nevertheless, with the expenses of construction and other contingencies of between £40,000 and £50,000, that sum would take years to recover.

Although Sir William Heygate didn't live long enough to see the pier completed, his fellow committee member General William Goodday Strutt survived to see the pier extended into deep water. This event marked the completion of the design set forth in the act of 1835 and, whatever the general's feelings towards the committee, the completion must have given the old soldier great satisfaction, especially as he could watch in peace the progress from his house on Marine Parade. Goodday Strutt never married and died at Tofts in little Baddow in 1848, aged 84.

PIER COMPANY BANKRUPT

Later audits revealed the true pier costs to date were £42,000. The outlay had ruined the Southend Pier Company and the remaining shareholders lost their money. In 1846, the Pier Company's largest creditor, the Public Works Loan Commissioners, demanded settlement of its loan. In consequence, the London auctioneers Shuttleworth and Sons were instructed to sell the pier. The prospectus ran,

"What was offered with the pier included a wharf, with sites for further buildings and two brick and timber tenements, the right to levy certain tolls on all vessels loading or unloading in Southchurch and up to the eastern boundary of Chalkwell Hall Farm in the parish of Prittlewell. A distance that extended four miles along the shore."

The sale took place on Friday August 28th 1846. The successful bidder was David Waddington who paid £17,000. David Waddington had a reputation for hard bargaining and cost cutting.

He was Vice-Chairman and later Chairman of the Eastern Counties Railway, which was reputed to have a poor safety record. Later Waddington went on to serve as the Member of Parliament for Maldon and then Harwich.

Sir Morton Peto

Waddington, though, soon sold the pier et al for £20,000, a profit of £3,000, to Sir Morton Peto of the Engineering Company, Brassey, Peto and Betts, who amongst many other projects had built the railway line from Gas-factory Junction, near Bow, to Southend.

In 1856 the London, Tilbury and Southend line opened its station in Southend which in turn changed the dynamics of travelling from London to Southend.

PIER TAKEN INTO PUBLIC OWNERSHIP

The pier remained in Brassey, Peto and Betts ownership for nearly 30 years. The owners were quite happy to bank the taking from tolls and admissions but showed little inclination to effect major improvements. All the while Southend's pier was gradually rotting away.

Salvation came in 1875 when ownership of the pier changed and became public property. After some hard bargaining the pier was purchased for just £12,000 by the Southend-on-Sea Local Board, the Local Government Authority of that date.

The purchase followed a fierce local debate amongst the ratepayers of Southend a year earlier. (See appendix, pier sale, page 117.) Two polls of ratepayers were conducted following heated and stormy meetings. The first poll was held over the 20th, 21st and 22nd May 1874 - to vote on the following resolution,

"That this meeting approves of the purchase of Southend Pier and property by the Local Board."

The result was 164 votes for and 14 against the resolution. However, there was a fierce ongoing campaign against Southend buying the pier during the summer and autumn of 1874. Southend was plastered with anti-pier posters and handbills and the local papers received a stream of angry letters objecting to the purchase.

The local board convened another public meeting on Friday 30th October 1874, under the chairmanship of George Vandervord who had succeeded James Heygate junior on his death. However, the Heygates still had a strong voice in local matters as James Unwin Heygate, the son of James Heygate junior, had been elected to the local board a year earlier and led the debate advocating the purchase of the pier. The meeting of October 30th was again long and bad tempered but nevertheless those present agreed to hold another ratepayer poll on the subject. This duly took place over the weekend of 20th – 22nd November with ballots collected on Monday 23rd November 1874.

The result was,

In favour of purchase **456**

Against **259**.

This result seemed to settle the matter.

It looked like the Local Board had assumed the vote would turn out the way it did – in favour of purchasing the pier - as on 12th November, a week before the ballot took place, the solicitor for the Local Board, William Gregson junior gave notice in the *Southend Standard* that the Local Board had applied to Parliament to authorise Southend to purchase the pier. (Details can be seen in the appendix page 128.)

With the ratepayer votes in favour and parliamentary approval secured, the Southend Local Board proceeded with the purchase for £12,000. The initial offer of £10,000 was turned down. The sale was completed on July 1st 1875 and Southend Pier became a public asset.

Although the Southend Pier Company had been ruined by the building of Southend Pier, James Heygate junior, despite his previous banking scandal, emerged as one the largest property owners in Southend. As mentioned above, his son James Unwin Heygate replaced him as a member of the Southend Local Board.

Rayleigh House on Marine Parade, General Strutt's Southend home, together with the shops that made up Strutt's Parade, were auctioned off in August 1865 and fetched £5,200.

In another twist in the saga was that George John Vandervord (1817 – 1888) was chairman of the Southend Local Board when the pier was taken into public ownership and did much to facilitate this happening. George had been a member of the local board from 1866 and became its chairman from 1873, following the death of James Heygate junior, and remained so until 1877.

What is perhaps ironic is that George Vandervord's father, also called George John (1792 – 1843) along with his brothers had vigorously opposed the Heygates' pier ambitions at every twist and turn during the 1830s. It is said the passage of time heals and so 40 years later the Vandervords and the Heygates worked in unison.

However, although the pier had become a public asset and purchased at a reasonable price with the benefit of a steady income stream, there was much still much work to do.

So, on this happy note, this is where the first part of the story of *The Struggle to Build Southend's First Pier* ends and the pier despite it many ups and down has remained in public ownership ever since.

The end of Southend Pier in deep water 1.3 miles from the shore

APPENDIX

1. THE SOUTHEND PIER COMPANY, THE SHAREHOULDERS

It has been difficult to get a list all the shareholders of the Southend Pier Company when it was set up in 1829, however eleven years later this was found in the *Chelmsford Chronicle* of 27th November 1840,

The Southend Pier Company

"The Act of Parliament for the formation of this Company passed the 14th May, 1829. The following are the names of the gentlemen who, as is customary, in order to obtain the act, undertook "at their own expense to effect the purposes" mentioned therein:—

Sir Thomas Maryon Wilson, Bart. Sir Claudius Stephen Hunter, Bart.; Elizabeth Babington, Anthony Bessant Barns, James Bayley, Wm. Butler, Thomas Bell, William Cotton, William Taylor Copeland, William Davis, William Drake, John Finlay, Robert Greenwood, Thomas Frost Gepp, - Gepp, James Gibson, James Heygate, James Heygate, the younger, Elizabeth Anne Heygate, Mathias Prime Lucas, Edward Longden Macmurdo, John Paynter, James Philpot, Major-General William Goodday Strutt, Robert Sutton, Robert Sutton, younger, James Sutton, and Andrew White, Clerk, with all other persons as shall from time to time, their respective successors, executor administrators, and assigns, as shall at any time be possessed of any share or shares in the undertaking".

There are three **Heygates** in the list, **James Heygate Senior**, **James Heygate** the younger and **Elizabeth Ann Heygate** (1788 – 1879). Elizabeth Anne Heygate was the daughter of James Heygate senior and Sarah (Unwin) Heygate, and sister (Sir) William Heygate Bart and James Heygate Jr.

2. PETITION OF JAMES WILSON VANDERVORD
of in the parish of Prittlewell in the county of Essex

Appeal in the House of Commons

"A Petition of **James Wilson Vandervord** of in the parish of Prittlewell in the county of Essex merchant and hoyman, was presented and read, setting forth,

That a Petition has been presented to the House for leave to bring in a Bill to amend an Act of the tenth George the Fourth c 49 for **Making and maintaining a Pier**, at or near Southend, in the parish Prittlewell in the county of Essex and for convenient approaches to and from the same; that Standing Orders of the House in relation to Piers and Roads have not been complied with in regard to said Petition and Bill; that inasmuch as the said Petition has reference to the making of Roads, a Map to have been deposited with the Clerk of the Peace on or before the 30th day of November last, together with a Book of Reference and a List of the Names of Owners or Occupiers whereas no such Map, List or Book of Reference has been so deposited; that by the Standing Orders of the House a like Plan or Map and an estimate of the proposed Expense, and also a Subscription List ought to have been deposited in the Private Bill Office, and a receipt for the same indorsed on the Petition, which the Petitioner shows has not been done, has an estimate of the probable time of completing the work and the probable expense of it been deposited there, nor have the requisite notices been given; and praying, That he may be heard by himself, his counsel, and witnesses, in support of his Petition and the House will enforce its Standing Orders and allow the said Bill to be proceeded in; or that the House will grant unto the Petitioner such further relief in the premises as the House shall deem fit and proper.

Ordered, That the said Petition do lie upon the Table."

"The said Petition was additionally supported by **Robert Scratton** of Southend in the county of Essex and **John Bayntun Scratton** of Milton otherwise Middleton Hall, in the parish of Prittlewell in the said county. The petition was presented and read to take taking notice of the Southend Pier Bill and that that they may be heard by themselves their counsel or agents, against certain parts thereof.

And the said Petitions were ordered to be referred to the Committee on the Bill; and the Petitioners heard, by themselves, their counsel or agents, upon their Petitions, if they think fit; and counsel heard in favour the Bill, against the said Petitions."

It was further debated on the 23rd July 1835. Parliament was very thorough and debated the bill stringently. Here is the debate.

"The House proceeded to take into consideration the Amendments made by the Lords to the Bill, entitled, An Act to explain and amend the Powers of an Act of his late Majesty King George the Fourth for making a Pier at Southend in the County of Essex: And the same were read and are as followeth:

Pr 2 1 20 Leave out from "Jetty" to But in line 26.

Pr 7 1 6 Leave out from whereas to it in Pr 8 1 4

Pr 8 1 9 Leave out same and insert tolls rates and duties authorized to be taken in respect of wares or merchandize due and payable in the manner directed by the said Act and in the same line and in line 10 after therefore insert further

Pr 15 Leave out from notwithstanding to and in Pr 19 1 7 Pr 21 1 11. After not insert Clause A CLAUSE A And be it further Enacted That when the said Pier or Jetty shall be completed as aforesaid the said Company shall, and they are hereby required at all times to maintain at the extremity thereof a good and sufficient light under such regulations as the Corporation of the Trinity House of Deptford Strand may from time to time direct

The Amendments as far as Pr 15 ult being read a second time were agreed to Pr 15 ult. The next Amendment which was to leave out from the word notwithstanding to and in Pr 19 being a Clause whereby power was given to issue public money for the purposes of the Act being read a second time; was agreed to the said Clause having been introduced in the Committee on the Bill, without the authority of this House, and without the usual forms in cases of granting power to issue public money having been complied with. Then the subsequent Amendments being read a second time were agreed to Ordered That Mr Hall Dare do carry the Bill to the Lords and acquaint them that this House hath agreed to Amendments made by their Lordships."

Captain Frederick Bullock (1778-1874), who acted as a surveyor for the Admiralty, boldly declared that he disapproved of the construction of any pier in the Thames but admitted he had not been supported by the Admiralty in this sweeping expression of opinion. The hearing lasted several days.

"The Committee heard evidence at wearisome length concerning the use made of the Harbour. It was admitted by the witnesses for the Company that very few vessels had unloaded there, the collector of Pier dues stating that not more than five barges had been there in the five years the Pier was opened, whilst it was admitted that the conveyors of the traffic, which was controlled by **Messrs Vandervord**, landed the goods in the way they had been accustomed to do before the Pier was built, viz., by running on to the shore and unloading at low water into carts. **Mr George Vandervord** said in this way he had loaded 500 quarters of corn in one day and delivered ten tons of goods. He had seen as many as forty wagons come down to the beach to load corn. A tendency to silt within the harbour was discussed, and it was said the decay of seaweed caused a smell which was noticeable from Royal Terrace.

The Commons Committee, before the hearing concluded, intimated that additional evidence was not required to establish the inutility (having no practical use) of the present work as a harbour."

3. BARGES OWNED AND SAILED BY THE VANDERVORDS OF SOUTHEND
showing details as known

ALMA

Spritsail - 41 Tons
Port - London - Registration Entry,Official No. 11950
Built in Lambeth in 1855
Owners : 1865-1904 J & G Vandervord & J Underwood
Joe Wiggins, Thundersley C'1911

ANN

Spritsail - 29 Tons Port - Faversham - Registration Entry - 1/1824
Port - Maldon - Registration Entry - 11/1847, Official No: 42572
Built at Limehouse in 1816
Dimensions (ft) 59.2 x 14.5 x 4.4, Signal Letters: TKJC
1847 James Vandervord, Southend
1853 Jas & Geo Murrell, Hockley
1865-75 Robt. Surridge, Limehouse

ASHLEY

Spritsail - 54 Tons,Port - London- Registration Entry -1804
Port - Faversham - Registration Entry - 1808
Port - Rochester - Registration Entry - 21/1816
Port - Maldon - Registration Entry - 6/1817
Port - London - Registration Entry - 1842
Port - Maldon - Registration Entry - 1843
Official No:
Built at Reading in 1804
Dimensions (ft) 59.6 x 17.5 x 5.7
Signal Letters:
Owners:
1817 Thomas Bannister, South Church, 1825 James Hills. Leigh
1833 Mark Martin, Leigh, 1843 James Wilson Vandervord, Southend

ASSISTANCE

Boomsail - 20 Tons Port - Maldon - Registration Entry - 17/1827
Official No: 11082 Built 1827
Dimensions (ft) 41 x 12 x 4.4
Owners:
1846 Elizabeth Meeson, Rochford
1865 Thos. Laslett, N. Shoebury
1874 George Vandervord, Southend
1883 George Woods, Southend
Condemned January 1810 in the High Court of the Admiralty

BETSEY

Barge - 54 Tons
Port - Maldon - Registration Entry - 10/1787
Port - Maldon - Registration Entry - . 2/1826
Port - London - Registration Entry - 1827
Built at London in 1770 .
Dimensions (ft) 54 x 16.4 x 4.1 Enlarged to 55.7 x 17.1 x 4.6
Owners:
1787 Capt Sam Cockerton, Prittlewell
1825 Abraham Vandervord, Southend
1826 James Vandervord, Southend
1827 James Heygate, Southend
1886 Broken Up

CERES

Barge - 66 Tons (Reduced to 42 Tons)
Port - Maldon - Registration Entry - 10/1807
Port - London - 1843 and 1849
Port - Harwich - 1883
Official No: 17820
Built at Colchester in 1807 by W. Stuttle
Dimensions (ft) 60.6 x 18 x 5.9 reduced to 60 x 15.9 x 5.5
Owner and skipper, 1807 Abraham Vandervord, Southend

DEERHOUND

Spritsail - 48 Tons
Port - Maldon - Registration Entry 9/1864, Official No: 50451
Built at Sittingbourne in 1864 by S. Taylor
Dimensions (ft) 73.5 x 18.2 x 4.8
Owners:
1864 [1] George & Emmanuel Vandervord, Southend
1895 William Bowman, Southen
1897 Alfred Vandervord, Southend - "sold at Auction by Messrs. J.C.
Hammond & Co., 77 Mark Lane London in connection with the
Estate of Messrs. G & E Vandervord sold on 17th Inst) for £351.5.0."
Wrecked on Grain Spit

DISPATCH

Square Stern Barge - 49 Tons
Port - Maldon - Registration Entry - 33/1786
Port - Maldon - Re-Registrated Entry - 29/1800 as Spritsail
Port - London - Transferred Registration Entry - 85/1804
Built at London in 1776, Dimensions (ft) 54.6 x 16.2 x 4.6
1800 Abraham Vandervord of Southend, Hoyman
Notes:
Based at Battlesbridge in 1786, Leigh in 1800

EFFORT

Square Sterned Barge
Port - Maldon - Registration Entry - 7/1887
Port - Maldon - Registration Entry - 19/1805
Built at Vauxhall in 1786, Dimensions (ft) 567 x 20 x 6.4
Owners:
1787 Philip Going, South Shoebury
17? William then Joseph Going, South Shoebury
1802 Capt Matthew Fisher, Shoebury & Ben Bannister, Gt. Wakering
1805 Abraham Vandervord & Capt John Hutchins, Southend

ELIZABETH

Spritsail - 50 Tons, Port -Wisbech - Registration Entry - 4/1840
Port - Maldon - Registration Entry 5/1853
Official No: 17403, Built at York in 1840
Dimensions (ft) 59 x 13.7 x 6
Owners:1853 George Vandervord (Hoyman) Southend & Ed.
Maddams & Thomas Laslett (Coal Merchant) Shoebury

EMILY

Spritsail - 32 tons
Port - Maldon - Registration Entry - 3/1875
Official No: 794, Built at Northfleet in 1844 by J. Wright
Dimensions (ft) 66.8 x 12 x 4.4
Owners:
1849 George Vandervord, Southend
1872 George Vandervord, Southend
1897 Alfred Vandervord, Southend - "sold by Messrs J. C. Hammond
& Co, 77 Mark Lane, London in connection with estate of Messrs G &
E Vandervord on 17th inst for £73.10.0"
1910 Broken Up

ESSEX FARMER

Spritsail - 50 Tons
Port - London - Registration Entry - 4/1856
Port - Maldon - Registration Entry - 1897
Official No: 11087, Built at Long Ditton in 1856 by Phillips
Dimensions (ft) 77.6 x 17.3 x 5.5
Owners:
1856 [1] George Vandervord, Southend
1882 George Vandervord, Southend
1895 Henry Thompson, Leigh on Sea
1896 sank in gale, but washed up on beach undamaged.

FACTOR

Spritsail - 84 Tons
Port - Rochester - Registration Entry - 8/1833
Port - London - Registration Entry - 38/1836
Port - Maldon - Registration Entry - 4/1853
Port - Maldon - Registration Entry - 3/1858
Official No: 26386
Built at Bankside in 1833 by D. White
Dimensions (ft) 63 x 17.4 x 5.2 - re-registered in 1836 as 61 x 14.5 x 5.7, then 72.5 x 18.1 x 5.7 in Maldon in 1858
Owners:
1833 [1] David Triton, Sheerness#
1853 R.J. Meeson & W. J. Meeson, Battlesbridge
1872 W. J. Meason, Rochford
1876 E. Brazier, Southend
1888 John Cowley at auction for £225, resold
1888 George Vandervord, Southend
1897 George F Vandervord, Southend (Managing Owner)
Foundered west Swin 1 Jan 1903 (Reg. Entry)

FARMER'S INCREASE

Square Stern Barge - 87 Tons
Port - Maldon - Registration Entry - 78/1786
Port - Maldon - Registration Entry - 17/1795 - Sloop rigged barge- 92 tons
Port - Ipswich - Registration Entry- 19 Oct 1798
Built at Vauxhall, Surrey in 1784
Dimensions (ft) 67.11 x 20 x 6
Owners:
1786 Daniel Heard of Southend in Prittlewell, mariner
1795 Abraham Vandervord (Hoyman) of Prittlewell
Masters: 1784 Daniel Heard,1787 Abram Vandervord via Heard
1790 John Sears via Vandervord, 1791 John Hutchin via Sears
1795 John Hutchin
1794 Hired by Admiralty as Hired Armed Vessel

FOUR SISTERS

Pink Stern Sloop - 60 Tons
Port - Transferred from Colchester - 32/1796
Port - Maldon - Registration Entry - 1801
Port - London - Registration Entry - 183/1803
Built at St Osyth in 1763
Owners: 1801 Abraham Vandervord, Southend Master mariner and
Christopher Parson of North Shoebury, Gent
Based at Leigh

GANNET

Spritsail - 50 Tons, Port - London - Registration Entry
Official No: 95453
Built at Limehouse in 1888 by H. Shrubsall
Dimensions (ft) 81 x 18.3 x 6
Owners:
1888 [1] Alfred Vandervord, Southend - "sold by Messrs J. C.
Hammond & Co, 77 Mark Lane, London from Estate of G & E
Vandervord on 17th Inst for £735.00"
1903 Edith Peters, Southend
1919-1923 S. J. Peters, Southend
1926 Smeed Dean, Murston (Rebuilt)
Lost. Floundered 9 Mar 1939 near West Buxey.

GEORGE CANNING

Spritsail - 69 Tons, Port - London - Registration Entry - 226/1826
Port - Maldon - Registration Entry - 8/1831
Built at Woolwich in 1825
Dimensions (ft) 64.6 x 17.7 x 4.10
Owners:
1831 James Bull, Lighterman, Woolwich
1831 Edwin Sumner, Gent, Southend
1836 Vandervoord, Southend
1890 William Bowman, Shoeburyness

GEORGE & ALFRED

Spritsail - 45 Tons, Official No: 42537, Built at Sittingbourne in 1862 by Taylor, Dimensions (ft) 75 x 19 x 6.5
Signal Letters: TKJD
Owners:
1862 George Vandervord, Southend
1881 George Vandervord, Southend
1897 Alfred Vandervord, Southend- "sold by Messrs J. C. Hammond & Co, 77 Mark Lane, London from Estate of G & E Vandervord on 17th Inst for £325.00"
1903 Dan Osborne, Faversham

IONA

Spritsail - 49 Tons,, Port - London
Official No: 67113, Built at Frindsbury in 1875 by Curel
Owners:
1875 [1] John Scott, Farmer, Wouldham 1895 Emanuel Vandervord, Southend - "sold by Messrs J. C.Hammond & Co, 77 Mark Lane, London from Estate of G & E Vandervord on 17th Inst for £412.00"
1904 to London Rochester Barge Co. One of the first barges to be fitted with a wheel

JANE

Spritsail - 57 Tons, Port - London - Registration Entry
Official No: 102828, Built at Sittingbourne in 1893 by White
Owners:
1904-1911[1] Alfred Vandervord, Southend
1923-1947 Everard, Greenhithe
Lost. Crushed by USS Titan in royal Albert Dock 1947 and Broken Up

JOHN EVELYN

Spritsail - 72 Tons, Port - London - Registration Entry
Official No: 91875, Built at Deptford in 1885 by Braby
Owners:1885 [1] Vandervord, Southend, Became a House Barge

LORD PALMERSTON

Spritsail - 42 Tons, Port - London - Registration Entry
Official No: 12916,Built at Lamberth in 1857
Owners:
1865-73 Underwood, Southend
1888 George & Alfred Vandervord, Southend - bought at auction £295
Lost. Floundered 9 Mar 1939 near West Buxey.

MARY & ELIZABETH

Barge - 60 Tons
1740's Geroge Richardson
1743 Abraham Vandervord, Southend -

MINERVA

Spritsail - 82 Tons, Port - Maldon- Registration Entry
Port - Maldon - Registration Entry - rebuilt in 1810 - 42 tons
Official No: 26501
Dimensions (ft) 65.11 x 19.2 x 5.10
Owners:
1811 Abraham Vandervord, Southend
1817 Thos Bullen & Abraham Markham, Southend - "sold by Abraham Vandervord's executors to Bullen & Markham"
1826 James Vandervord, Southend
1851 James Wilson Vandervord, Southend

PITSEA

Barge- 40 Tons
Owners:
1767 John Cousins, Southend
Masters: 1777 Abraham Vandervord (aged 18 years of age)
John Cousins was Abraham's stepfather from the age of 8 years

RACHEL & JULIA

Spritsail - 53 Tons, Port - London - Registration Entry - 44/1873
Official No: 68392, Built at Miltonin 1873 by R. Shrubsall
Dimensions (ft) 75 x 18.8 x 5.3
Owners:
1873 [1] Howard, Great Wakering
1895 Vandervord, Southend - (as 41ft)
1904-1918 Mrs. Alice Rawlingson, London

RATHBALE

Spritsail - 58 Tons, Port - London - Registration Entry
Official No: 106520, Built at Erith in 1896
Owners:1896 Vandervord, Southend
1904 Beckwith, Colchester
1911-1923 Goldsmith, Grays
An Iron Barge

ROVER

Spritsail - 37 Tons, Port - London - Registration Entry
Official No: 54698.Built at Millwall in 1865 by Hartnoll
Re-built at Murson in 1927 by Smeed
Owners:
1865 [1] Hartnoll & Surridge, Millwall
1885 Vandervord, Southend
1895-1904 William Stafford, Shoeburyness
1911 William Theobald, Leigh
Lost anchor & chain in December 1914 gale. Crew taken off and
barge washed ashore at Herne Bay, 1918 Vessel disposed of

ROYAL OAK

Cutter (Boomsail rigged) sloop raid barge - 91 Tons rebuilt to 59 tons
Port - London - Registration Entry - 17/1798
Port - Maldon - Registration Entry - 18/1798
Port - Maldon - Registration Entry - 95/1825
Port - London - Registration Entry - 1826
Port - Maldon - Registration Entry - 10/1847
Official No: 905, Built at Limehouse in 1798
Re-built in 1825 to flat bottom square stern
Dimensions (ft) 71 x 20 x 5.11 rebuilt to 70.2 x 19.10 x 6.5 to 59 tons
Owners:
1798 Abraham Vandervord, Southend in Prittlewell, Hoyman
1817- "transferred by Jas Dixon (executor of A.Vandervord's will) whole vessel to William Heard Vandervord, George Vandervord and James Wilson Vandervord, all of Southend, Hoymen
1843 8 June - in the will of George John Vandervord "hereby direct my son George Vandervord shall have director and management of the barge called the *Royal Oak*
1846 George Vandervord, Southend
Masters: 1798, John Hutchin, 1811, Jas Rowley via Abm Markwell
Based at Leigh, 1894 dismasted
'The oldest barge in the 1893 Mercantile Navy List, the Maldon *Royal Oak*, and still with the Vandervords of Southend almost a century later.

SUSANNAH

Flat Bottomed Sailing Barge- 50 Tons
Port - Maldon - Registration Entry - 4/1803
Port - Maldon - Registration Entry - 7/1808 - Flat bott. Square Stern
Official No: 26601, Built at Lambeth (Surrey) in 1789
Dimensions (ft) 56 x 16.2 x 4.6
Owners
1789 [1] Abraham Vandervord, Southend, mariner
1803 Abraham Vandervord, Southend
Based at Leigh 1803, Maldon 1808

WATERLOO

Boomsail - 73 Tons
Port - Maldon - Registration Entry - 15/1816
Port - London - Registration Entry - 1837
Port - Maldon - Registration Entry - 3/1853
Official No: 24595, Built at Millwall in 1816 by R. Barnett
Re-built at Murson in 1927 by Smeed
Dimensions (ft) 64.5 x 18.9 x 5.5 and 63.4 x 18.7 x 6 in 1825
Owners:
1816 [1] Abraham Vandervord, Southend
1817 Thomas Bullen, Southend (William Vandervord - Master)
1827 William Vandervord, Southend
1852 William Vandervord, Southend
1853 James Wilson Vandervord, Southend
1853 Re-registered Maldon, shown as Southend Hoy Barge

WEST KENT

Spritsail - 45 Tons, Port - London - Registration Entry
Official No: 29338, Built at Deptford in 1865
Signal Letters: QFLT
Owners:
1865 Smith, Deptfond
1861 George Vandervord, Southend
1894 Alfred Vandervord, Southend
1904 William Baker, Southend
1911 William Theobald, Leigh
1881 In January this Barge smashed through Southend Pier. "The West Kent which had been unloading timber in the harbour, was swept bodily under the pier, a large part of which was washed away, marooning the look-out till he was later relieved by boat. The *West Kent* was repaired and still trading till 1925"

4. PIER EXTENSION SPECIFICATIONS

Courtesy of *The Surveyor, Engineer, and Architect, 1843-01-01: Vol 4 Issue 47.*
Lead Architect
Mr. James Simpson, V.P. Inst. C.E.

"The pier is to be constructed partly with cast-iron piles and partly with timber piles, to which the platforms, resting-places, landing- places, and stairs are to be fixed.

Datum Line. (this is a standard of comparison or point of reference). The top of the floor or platform of the pier head, and the top of the floor of the gangway or road of the extension of the pier, are to be level throughout, the datum line of such level being 12 inches above the upper surface or floor at the face or termination of the platform of the present pier.

Pier Head. The whole of the piles and timber connected with the present pier head or lighthouse platform is to be constructed with 40 timber piles, resting in and fixed to 40 cast-iron piles, and to be protected by 18 fender piles, finished with heads for mooring ropes, and a fender piece in front of each.

The lower platform of the pier head is to be constructed with planks supported on beams secured to the piles and finished with railing and one flight of stairs and rails to communicate with the middle platform.

The middle platform is to extend entirely round and across the pier head, and to be constructed with planks supported on beams secured to the piles, and finished with railing and two flights of stairs and rails to communicate with the upper platform.

The upper platform is to extend over the entire pier head, having two openings for the stairs to the middle platform. It is to be constructed of planks supported on beams secured to the piles and finished with railing.

Centre Line. The centre line of the platform of the gangway or road is to be straight, and direct from the centre of the present lighthouse platform to the centre of the termination or face of the present pier.

Gangway or Road. The first bay, or No. 1, a length of 20 feet of the floor of the gangway or road from the pier head northwards, is to commence

12 feet 9 inches wide, and finish 8 feet 9 inches wide, with 4 fender piles and waling.

The next 34 piles of 28 feet each, that is, from No 2 – 35, inclusive, or a length of 952 feet, of thereabouts of the floor of the gangway or road, is to be 8 feet 9 inches wide.

The next or 36th bay, or a length of 16 feet 10 inches, is to be a resting place, with the floor of its platform, including the gangway or roadway 18 foot 5 inches wide.

Gangway or Road. The next 35 bays, of 28 feet each, that is, from Nos. 37 to 71 inclusive, or a length of 980 feet or thereabouts of the floor of the gangway or road, is to be 8 feet 9 inches wide.

Resting Place. The next, or 72nd bay, or a length of 16 feet 10 ½ inches, is to be a resting place, with the floor of its platform including the gangway or 18 feet 5 inches wide.

Gangway or Road. The next 17 bay, of 28 feet each, that is, from Nos. 73 to 89 inclusive, or a length of 476 feet or thereabouts of the floor of the gangway or road, is to be 8 feet 9 inches wide.

Resting Place. The next, or 111th bay, or a length of 16 feet 10 ½ inches, is to be a resting place, with the floor of its platform, including the gangway or road is 18 feet 5 inches wide.

Gangway or Road. The next 35 bays of 28 feet each, that is, from Nos. 112 to 146 inclusive, or a length of 980 feet or thereabouts of the floor of the gangway or road, is to be 8 feet 9 inches wide.

The before-mentioned 111 bays, Nos. 1 to 111 inclusive from the pier head, are to be constructed with 242 timber piles, resting in and fixed to 242 cast-iron piles, with 2 cast-iron fitted keys to each. The next 66 bays, that is, from Nos. 112 to 177 inclusive, are to be constructed with 136 timber piles, shod with iron.

The whole of the piles of the bays are to be secured with cross- braces, and the entire length of the gangway or road is to be formed of planks fixed to the longitudinal beams, which are to be supported on sills and templet caps, secured to the pile heads with wrought-iron straps, keys, bolts, nuts, and plates, and the whole is to be finished on each side with permanent railing.

Cast-iron Piles. The cast-iron piles are to be square outside and inside, the thickness of the metal being uniform, except where otherwise shown, with a projecting band at top; at the depth of 5 feet 1 inch from the top inside of the piles, there is to be a flange seat projecting from the inner surface, to sustain the driving plates, and the bottoms of the piles are to be cast with cutting edges; each pile is to have two key-ways, and to be fitted with two cast-iron keys and a driving-plate ; part of the piles are to be cast with double and part with single brackets.

Fir Timber Piles.—All the iron piles are to be lowered, set, and driven with punching timbers, to prevent the necessity of using the permanent timber piles for that purpose; the 282 timber piles which are to be fixed to the iron piles to form the pier head, and the 111 outer bays of the pier, are to be of fir; the lower ends of the timber for a length of 5 feet are to be wrought and fitted into the cast-iron piles, the ends squared to bear equally on the driving piles, and previously to be driven in; the timber is to be charred and tarred; the space within the piles above the shore is to be filled with concrete, and the inside of the heads of the iron piles cleaned out and perfectly dried; after the timber piles are driven into the cast-iron piles, the mortices are to be cut, and the cast-iron piles driven in and rivetted.

Oak Timber Piles—The 136 timber piles before mentioned are to be of oak, and each shod with a wrought iron shoe, and driven to a depth varying from 8 feet to 8 feet 6 inches into the ground or shore.

Fender Piles. The fender piles, 34 in number, are to be of fir, and each driven with a wrought iron shoe to a depth of from 9 to 10 feet into the ground or shoe, being previously to driving hooped, charred, tarred, and scupper-nailed over the entire surface, from the level of the top of the cast-iron piles to the depth of at least 3 feet.

Resting Place. The next, or 147th bay, or a length of 16 feet 104 inches, is to be a resting place, with the floor of its platform, including the gangway or road, 18 feet 5 inches wide.

Gangway or Road. The next 30 bays of 28 feet each, that is, from Nos. 148 to 177 inclusive, or a length of 840 feet or thereabouts of the floor of the gangway or road, is to be 8 feet 9 inches wide.

The before-mentioned 111 bays, Nos. 1 to 111 inclusive from the pier head, are to be constructed with 242 timber piles, resting in, and fixed to 242 cast-iron piles, with 2 cast-iron fitted keys to each. The next 66 bays, that is, from Nos. 112 to 177 inclusive, are to be constructed with 136 timber piles, shod with iron.

The whole of the piles of the bays are to be secured with cross-braces, and the entire length of the gangway or road is to be formed of planks fixed to the longitudinal beams, which are to be 2 gen on sills and templet caps, secured to the pile heads with wrought-iron straps, keys, bolts, nuts, and plates, and the whole is to be finished on each side with permanent railing.

Cast-iron Piles. The cast-iron piles are to be square outside and inside, the thickness of the metal being uniform, except where otherwise shown, with a projecting band at top; at the depth of 5 feet 1 inch from the top inside of the piles, there is to be a flange seat projecting from the inner surface, to sustain the driving plates, and the bottoms of the piles are to be cast with cutting edges; each pile is to have two key-ways, and to be fitted with two cast-iron keys and a driving-plate; part of the piles are to be cast with double and part with single brackets.

Fir Timber Piles. All the iron piles are to be lowered, set, and driven with punching timbers, to prevent the necessity of using the permanent timber piles for that purpose; the 282 timber piles which are to be fixed to the iron piles to form the pier head, and the 111 outer bays of the pier, are to be of fir; the lower ends of the timber for a length of 5 feet are to be wrought and fitted into the cast-iron piles, the ends squared to bear equally on the driving piles, and previously to be driven in; the timber is to be charred and tarred; the space within the piles above the shore is to be filled with concrete, and the inside of the heads of the iron piles cleaned out and perfectly dried; after the timber piles are driven into the cast-iron piles, the mortices are to be cut, and the cast-iron piles driven in and rivetted.

Oak Timber Piles. The 136 timber piles before mentioned are to be of oak, and each shod with a ht-iron shoe, and driven to a depth varying from 8 feet to 8 feet 6 inches into the ground or shore.

Fender Piles. The fender piles, 34 in number, are to be of fir, and each driven with Tite lene on to Je pay vag ena (some of the print is unclear) 10 feet into the ground or, being previously to drive; charred, tarred, and nailed over the pee fer tng owe (again unclear), the scupper-level of the top of the cast-iron piles to the depth of at least 3 feet below the surface of the ground or shore. The fender pieces are to be of oak, securely fastened to the fender piles with jagged spikes.

Braces, Sills, & c. The braces, sills, chocks, cleats, templet caps and keys for scarfs are to be of oak and secured to the main piles with wrought-iron straps and spikes, keys, bolts, nuts, and plates.

Longitudinal Beams. The longitudinal beams are to be of fir, the outer sides of the chain beams to be wrought and planed, and to be in as long lengths as possible, and where necessary, they are to be scarfed together and fixed in such a way that no two scarfs or joining's of the outside main beams shall be directly opposite to each other.

Flooring and Platforms. The flooring and platforms are to consist of parallel oak planks laid with spaces of half an inch between them, securely spiked to the longitudinal beams, and to be wrought and planed on the upper side and left with a fair and even surface.

Stairs. The stairs for the pier head and landing places are to be of oak, the strings fastened together and secured to the piles with wrought-iron straps and bolts.

Railing. The railing is to consist of oak posts, secured to the longitudinal beams with wrought-iron straps, bolts, nuts, and plates, on three fir horizontal rails, the whole to be wrought and planed, the panels being filled up with vertical wrought-iron bars let into the middle and bottom rails; four of the bars in each bay are to be made with collars to rest on the centre rail, and with screwed ends and nuts to secure the top and bottom rails, and the entire railing finished with oak capping.

Painting, &c. The whole of the wrought-iron straps, keys, plates, bolts, and nuts to be painted four times in oil, and finished a black colour; the under-side of the floor and platforms and the inner longitudinal beams, and the whole of the timber below the level of the top of the diagonal braces, and the iron piles from the level of 5 feet above the driving end, are to be covered with two coats of pitch and tar mixed together in equal quantities; and all joints and scarfs throughout the work, as well as the part of the wooden piles driven into the iron, are to be covered in a similar manner previously to their being put together; the whole of the timber above the level of the top of the diagonal braces that is not pitched and tarred as above, as well as the wrought-iron railing after fixing, is to be painted four times in oil, and finished of such a plain stone colour as may be directed.

Braces and Mooring Posts. Diagonal braces and additional mooring posts will be required at the pier head and landing place, and these are to be fixed and secured with wrought-iron work in such places and in such manner as the engineer shall direct after these and stairs are completed. All such additional diagonal races and mooring posts are to be considered as extra works and paid for according to rates and prices to be stated in a schedule annexed to the tender.

Bed of River. The levels of the bed of the river and shore being variable, the lines on the drawings which refer to such levels have been delineated from drawings made in November 1842.

Tides. The levels of spring and neap tides marked on the drawings are from observations made in the months of April and May.

MATERIALS.

Cast Iron. The iron piles are to be cast in dry sand moulds, and the whole of the cast-iron work to be from cold-blast iron of a good tough quality, and not inferior to No. 2 Pig, second making.

Wrought Iron. The wrought iron is to be of the best scrap iron, and not inferior to bars.

Fir Timber. The fir is to be new Memel or Dantzic timber of approved quality, free from sap, shakes, and dead knots, and all other imperfections.

Oak Timber. The Company has about 500 loads of oak timber lying contiguous to the pier at Southend, which the contractor is to pardinde at £5 5s. per load, and to use in the work such ions of it as are perfectly sound, and free from sap, shakes, dead knots, and all other imperfections.

Present Lighthouse Platform. Such of the timber in the present lighthouse platform as is perfectly sound, and free from sap, shakes, and all other imperfections, is to be used in such parts of the work as may be directed by the Company's engineer.

Concrete. The concrete is to be composed of one part of good fresh-burnt stone lime pounded, and seven parts of clean, sharp, river gravel, mixed with a sufficient quantity of fresh water.

Pitch and Tar. The pitch is to be the best Swedish pitch, and the tar the best Stockholm tar, and each approved of before mixed.

Paint. The paint is to be composed of the best white lead and linseed oil, coloured as may be required. Pier Extension Specifications 1844.

5. COURT CASE EXTRACTS

Perhaps the most significant case in the long running dispute on the collection of pier tolls was the Southend Pier Company against Messrs. Vandervord, barge owners. This was heard at Wickford Castle on the 13th August 1838 and reported in the *Chelmsford Chronicle* of 17th August 1838, and repeated in the *Essex Herald* of 21st August 1838. The hearing at the Sessions lasted for the unprecedented two days. Extracts from the hearing follow.

The Southend Pier Company against the Messrs. Vandervord, barge owners, for having refused to pay the dues, and for resisting the Company's collector when he attempted to make distress for the sum due.

Mr. Disney, Chairman and convicting justice,
Magistrates present-**The Rev T. Brooksby**. Chairman. And **J. R. S. Phillips. Esq**.

SOUTHEND PIER DUES

Mr. Knox appeared for the Company, and **Mr. Price** for the defendants. The first information was against **George John De Vandervord**.

Mr. Knox, in opening the case, said, it was a matter of considerable regret, that after the proceedings to last year, they should be again assembled; for he had and hoped that the parties would have found the conduct they then pursued was as little defensible as it was little profitable. This was a matter for their consideration; and he would throw out that if there were any persons in the background supporting this conduct, they would make themselves liable to proceedings much more serious than those adopted against the Messrs. Vandervord.

Mr. Price said, he could assure Mr. Knox there was no such thing — nothing of the kind; and one of the complaints of the defendants was that the whole of the expenses fell to them.

Mr. Knox said, he was happy that assertion had been made, because persons taking up the matter from prejudice, or any other motive, would make themselves liable to penalties more severe than any under this Act of Parliament

The act passed, and there was no doubt the undertaking would be beneficial to the public generally, and especially to those who resided at Southend, or were in the habit or going there, though some individuals might look on the undertaking with jealousy of feeling, which was felt by the parties now before them, and led to that long-continued resistance which the Company complained.

The parties opposed to the measure had due advantage from that circumstance: it gave them an opportunity, if they thought fit to avail themselves of it, of again making their representations to the Legislature, and they opposed the Bill at enormous expense, - in fact, by fixing on the Company such expense as they have done, they did very much to prevent the completion of the undertaking to the extent contemplated.

"From and after the time the said piers or jetties or either of them shall be so far formed and completed that ships or vessels may be able to lade or unlade, take on board, or put on shore any goods or merchandise at the same respectively, such pier or jetty not less than one hundred and fifty feet in length and containing a surface not less than seven thousand and five hundred square feet."

They would observe that the Act did not say when the Pier was in a fit state then the right should arise, because that would have left it indefinite and open to disputes to what was a fit state, but it provided the state when duties should be payable. When it was carried out 150 feet, with surface of 7,500 square feet, and vessels could load and unload on it, then the duties were to be paid. Now he should show them by the evidence of the engineer that it could be used to load and unload goods, and that contained the measurement required by Act Parliament – that it had been carried out 277 feet, almost twice the length required, and instead of 7,500 square feet it contained 9,290.

The Act then went to say,

"Every master of every ship, vessel, boat, or other craft who shall lade or unlade, take on board or discharge, any goods, wares merchandize, within said parish of Southchurch, and such part of the said parish of Prittlewell as extends from the eastern boundary of the parish of Southchurch to the eastern boundary of the estate called Chalkwell Hall Farm, shall pay to the said company in regard thereof the several rates or duties mentioned in the schedule hereunto annexed, set down in figures against same respectively."

It would occur to them that this provision was included in the clause to prevent an evasion of the Act, and therefore it gave the duties to the Company whether the goods were landed on the Pier or not, if they were landed within a certain limit. He **(Mr. Knox)** should show that the goods on which the Company claimed the duties were landed within the limits.

They were now proceeding under two Acts of Parliament, and it was necessary he should state to them why. The first Act did not call on the parties to account of the goods put on board, but Company power to distress if the dues were under £2O. if over by action at law; but on consideration the point, with the assistance the most eminent lawyers of the day, they came to the conclusion that they could say "we will wait till it is over £2O, and then proceed by action."

It was the intention give a cheap remedy before a Magistrate, and though he was sorry that they could not obtain the decision of a higher Court, he did not see that the defendants should complain. It was necessary that the Company should know the amount of duties which ought to be paid, otherwise they would distrain in the dark, and when it became necessary to go to the Legislature to correct the word "not" a clause was introduced on that subject. The sixth section of the new act said:

"That the master, owner, or other person or persons having the care of any ship, or any other vessel in respect of whose cargo, or any part thereof, any tolls, rates, or duties are made payable under and by virtue of said recited Act, shall give to the collector or collectors, of the said tolls, rates, or duties, or any other officer or officers to be appointed for such purpose by the said company of proprietors, at the place or places where he or they attend for that purpose, a true and just account in writing, signed by the master, owner, or other person or persons having the care of each ship or vessel, of the quantities, qualities, and weight of the goods and other things to each such ship vessel, from whence brought, and where same are intended be landed; and the goods other things contained in any such ship or vessel shall be liable to the payment of each of the said tolls, rates, or duties, then such master, owner, or other person or persons shall specify the quantities liable to the payment of each of the said tolls, rates or duties; and in case he or they shall neglect or refuse to give such an account, or shall refuse to produce his or their invoice or bill of lading to the officer demanding the same, or shall, with intent to avoid the payment the said tolls, rates, duties, or give a false account, or shall deliver out any part of such lading or goods at any other place or places than what is or are mentioned in such invoice or bill of lading, every person so shall forfeit and pay to the said company a sum equal to twice the amount of the tolls, rates, or duties payable in respect the goods, wares, or merchandize which shall not have been duly accounted for, in leu of the single amount of tolls, rates, and duties made payable by the said recited Act.

There were also recounts of information charging **Mr. Vandervord** with resisting the officer in making the distress, the precise and legal definition of the first offence was a refusal to account under the Act of Parliament, and he should show them six several occasions, three when goods were loaded and three when they were unloaded, when tolls became due.

This was an offence as the clause read, -

"That in case any person persons shall resist or make forcible opposition against any person or persons employed in the due execution of this act, or shall assault any surveyor or agent, or any collector or collectors of tolls, in the execution of his or their office or offices, or shall forcibly pass through the toll gates or bars to be erected by virtue of this act without having paid the said tolls, every such person shall for every such offence forfeit and pay any sum not exceeding five pounds."

He would conclude his statement with the one observation with respect to the sums sought to be recovered. If the Magistrate was satisfied that the Pier was in such a state as authorised the Company to receive the duties, he had no discretion as to the amount of the penalty, because the last Act required that it should be single duty; but with respect to the three last charges for resisting the officer, he had power to mitigate it. As, however, proceedings were last year taken against these parties, he did say that unless the full penalty was inflicted. It was vain to make application to the Legislature for an Act of this description; and he would repeat that the only reason why the Pier had not been made so convenient as it might have been, was because persons like **Mr. Vandervord** had taken the course they had done.

William Richard Morris, a civil engineer, stated that he planned and measured a portion of the works before the Pier was erected, and he had measured the existing Pier. Its length on that part used for landing goods was 277 feet; he had measured the whole of the other part of the Pier but had not the account with him; he should suppose the whole length from the shore was 1,400 or 1,500 feet; it exceeded 1,400. He measured the superficies (surfaces) of the lower platform, and found it contained 9,290 square feet. In his judgment the Pier was so far formed and completed that ships could load and unload goods and merchandise on it. The lower connected with the upper platform and he should call them indiscriminately a pier or jetty. He had had considerable experience loading and unloading ships, though not on that spot, and had no doubt that 200 tons of coals might brought up there, but a great deal would depend on the build of the vessel; any vessel that could float there might unload.

Mr. Knox said, some vessels a heavy burthen could not come within two miles, - the question was whether vessels that could come up there could unload at the Pier.

Mr. Price said, that was not the question—it was whether a vessel, that could not unload at the Pier, would be liable to the penalties if it went into deeper water to unload.

Mr. Knox replied that the intention was to enable vessels such a burthen as traded with Southend to load there, otherwise they might say that a man of war should unload its guns there.

Mr. Price said, under that Act a man of war should unload there.

Mr. Disney said, it appeared him that the Company were to furnish a pier that would enable such vessels as would float there to load and unload: they did not undertake to make any alteration in the water.

Mr. Price proceeded to contend that if the "Royal Oak" went to the Pier, being 93 tons burthen, she would often be detained for want of sufficient depth of water, and defendant's business would be standing still. If he could use the accommodation of the Pier, he would be very willing to pay for it.

Mr. Knox. If you can show that **Mr. Vandervord** cannot make use of the Pier that will be an answer.

After some further discussion on this point between the Counsel, **Mr. Disney** said, there was no power to deepen the water —the question was, could vessels capable of using that water come and unload there.

Wm. Henry King, Collector of Customs at the port of Leigh, produced the clearances of the *Royal Oak* to show that goods liable to the duties were put on board on the days stated in the information.

John Ingram, a Toll Collector of the Pier Company, proved that he was on duty on the days named, and that he saw quantities of corn, which he specified, potatoes, and other goods, put on board the *Royal Oak*. He had seen vessels loading and unloading at the Pier, at what was called the lower platform and there was difficulty in loading and unloading. He should not suppose that **Mr. Vandervord's** vessels would find any difficulty—there never had been a vessel there yet that had not been able to load and unload there. Cross-examined. He had seen a vessel of 110 tons unload there; it was at high water, and she got away again as soon as she unloaded. She drew 9 feet 8 inches water. He should think at the last spring tide there was ten feet and a half of water, and vessels coming in could get out next tide. The vessel he had mentioned was the "Ruby" - she came in on the 28th of March last. A vessel of 110 tons would have had more convenience to load at the Pier than lower down; but if she had been full laden, she would have had wait till the tide came in again. This vessel could not have come in if it had been neap tide, nor at any part of the shore at the common working places. There was a small difference from the Pier to where **Mr, Vandervord** unloads, and a vessel might at times unload there when it could not unload at the Pier. If the Pier had been lower down larger vessels could not have loaded there.

Re-examined. I have seen vessels larger than **Vandervord's** load and unload at the Pier at different times.

John Patterson, toll-collector, also said had seen larger vessels than Mr. Vandervord's unload there. The *Ruby* was the largest he had seen there, but there had been others that drew as much water. Witness called at **Mr. John George Vaudervord's** on the 5th of May to demand the tolls, and he then went on board the *Royal Oak* to make a distress for them; he was about to take a coil of rope, but the defendant resisted his taking it by standing on it, and he was assisted by his sons. On the 9th of May, and the 16th of June, the same thing happened.

Cross-examined. The vessels that came to the Pier to unload were 50, 60, or 70, tons; they had had one of 97 tons, the *John and Eliza*, which came in full laden with chalk; she drew about 7 feet 2 inches; a sharp vessel of that size could not land there. At low neap tide there was about six feet water there. There were hands went out to pull the *John and Eliza* in, but the master would rather have been without them; she went away with 1,200 or 1,400 sacks of potatoes. Witness had no hesitation in saying that this was the best shipping place on the whole shore.

Mr. Price again observed that any vessels ought to be able to unload at the Pier.

Mr. Knox said, to do that they must have had a pier 3,000 feet to carry them into the deep water.

Mr. Price. If you had an Act of Parliament to enable you to open oysters with a rolling pin you would not be able to do so. Witness said, at high tide when they had 10 feet and a half water at the lower platform, the difference the extreme south end of the Pier was a foot or fourteen inches.

Cross-examined. When he went on board the *Royal Oak* the tolls were refused, and he said he must distrain; defendant called his workmen and sons to put their feet on the coil and said he should not take it away. They did not at the time ask him for his warrant of authority; he did not on that occasion produce his authority. Witness said that he could positively swear that his authority was not demanded.

The general authority which the witness held from the Company was produced.

Mr. Price here took an objection to the form of the information: it stated that the defendant resisted the officer in the execution of the Act, but he contended that it ought to have gone on and described the specific offence; by stating that on such a day he resisted him by putting his foot on coil of rope.

Mr. Knox contended that resisting the officer was the offence created by the Act, and putting his foot on the rope was matter of evidence. The information had closely followed the words of the Act, and that was sufficient.

After a long discussion on this point, the Chairman said, he saw no objection to the information. This was the case in support of the information.

Mr. Price then addressed the Court in a speech of great length. He was sorry, he said, that certain persons had been alluded to as being in the background and hoped he had relieved the parties from that assertion: there was no such thing; on the contrary, one principal and material ground of complaint was that the expense was made to fall **on Mr. Vandervord**. They wished for a decision in this matter, which had been too long in dispute, for it was injurious to a man in trade who got his bread by the sweat of his brow, to he brought in this way from home. He thought it a hard thing that the defendant had been called on means of an information to try a large legal question of great importance to the community, for he denied what had been stated that there were no other means of recovering this money than by this paltry mode of proceeding. It was unpleasant for the Magistrate to sit there and decide between the parties, but he was sure which way his duty would incline him; for unless these tolls were really due and from **Mr. Vandervord**, there was not the least pretence for these proceedings. He did not like double charge of this description in the information; they ought to have been separated, and the non-production of the account made different charges. It was for the Company to make out the claim to the satisfaction of the Magistrate—it was for them to make out that boats could load at the Pier, for if they could not load there, how could it be said that they ought to do so. Would it be said that the defendant was to do impossibilities by bringing in his barges when they could not go for want of water, or that they should go in when they could not get out again? It was better that **Mr. Vandervord** should do anything rather than be impeded in his daily business; and if he could avail himself of the Pier he would be very glad to so.

He contended that according to the Act the Western steam-boat, touching at Southend, must unload its cargo at the Pier; and suppose **Mr Vandervord** was Captain of the *Great Western* and chose to freight with corn, was he to be told that he was obliged to go there with this vessel of impracticable burthen? He must press it to this extremity, for if **Mr. Vandervord** was liable to pay tolls, every vessel which landed two-pennyworth of tobacco or cigars, must go to the Pier. Would the Company go as far as that?

Mr. Knox. Yes.

Mr. Price continued—Vessels of this description could not land their cargoes there, but the Company said—"We don't care whether it can be done—here is an Act of Parliament and you must do it." They required Mr. Vandervord to land his goods there, and they said, "If your vessel loaded with taxable commodities is too large to land there, yet because we have built a pier you shall pay us for it," although it was proved that sharp bottomed vessels of this size could not get into the place enclosed as a harbour, if we proved that **Mr. Vandervord's** vessel could not float there, any more than it could do on a saucer, was not that an answer to the case?—for he maintained that if they had not built such a Pier as would let in any vessel that would be glad to come in, they had no right to the tolls. There was no limit in the Act as to the size of the vessels, although if it intended it could have been done, for they knew what the water was capable of; and putting it on this footing, they were bound to show that **Mr. Vandervord** could land his goods there more conveniently than he could the other place. The Company's Act being the law of the land, he admitted as far as within their power they were bound obey it; but when they were called on to answer for an infraction of its provisions, they ought to show that, wilfully and knowingly, and with capacity to obey they had unlawfully infringed its enactments —in fact had attempted to cheat the Company.

The whole of his client's opposition to the bill, expensive as it had been, must show his sincerity, for it proved that he did not go to law for a vain fancy or humour, or from the worst passions of malignity and malice, but he was endeavouring to protect the properly which he derived from the sweat of his honest brow. It was said that the opposition of **Mr. Vandervord** had prevented the Company carrying the undertaking out to the extent contemplated; but had he nothing to complain of? had he no complaint to make when they saw his Learned Friend, of much greater experience than him (Mr. P.) brought down to conduct the case; and with this influence and talent arrayed against him, he threw himself on the powerful protection of the Court, and if the Magistrates would not protect him, he need not say, "God have mercy on us," for God could not.

He asked, if on the evidence which they had heard, they could convict the well-known **Vandervords** of Southend? Were there no seamen in Southend who could be brought to prove the facts of the case? why had they not been brought forward to prove that **Mr. Vandervord** could unload his goods at the Pier? **Mr. Morris** slated that he had had no experience in loading and unloading goods at this place, and would they not in justice and in mercy expect that better evidence should be produced before they put the defendants to the expense and trouble of an appeal to the Session?

They said— "Give us a Pier we can use, and we shall be glad to so," — that he was authorised to state, on the part of his clients, and let them, then not to be charged with infractions of the law.

According to the act he contended that they must show that they had a practical Pier for all and every vessel, and if not, they were not entitled to the dues they demanded. The defendants were units in the great sum of the public, and they had a right to the accommodation which the public had a right to demand of the Pier Company; and if the Pier was not in a state to be used by them, there was no right to demand toll of persons who did not land their goods there.

The Learned Gentleman then repeated his objection to the form of the information and contended that the collector was not at the time in the execution of the Act, as stated, though he was in the execution of an office of which he was appointed to under the Act.

A conversation here took place between the parties, and it was endeavoured to affect an accommodation. **Mr Knox** said the Company compounded for the dues with others and there was a disposition to compound with **Messrs Vandervord** in the same way.

Mr Wood, on part of the Company, proposed that **Messrs Vandervord** should pay £40 a year for each for the dues, and half the dues on other articles.

Mr Price offered £15 a year for the corn dues, but an arrangement could not be affected.

Mr Vandervord, brother of the defendant, was then examined. He said that the Pier would admit small craft of 30 or 40 tons to load and unload, but they must be flat-bottomed. The maximum that could get up there would be 40 tons. At a deep spring tide at the tip-top he had seen a schooner in there, but it had great difficulty to get up.

If the *Royal Oak* got in and was fully loaded, in all probability it would have to lay a long while before it got out again; but if it was at its old moorings opposite the Ship, where it had been place for 120 years, the difference would be considerable, for they had 2 feet 2 or 2 feet 4 inches more water there than they had at the Pier.

When the vessel was loaded it was time to proceed to market, and if they were detained for want of water, they would lie at the mercy of dealers to throw the corn up when they got to London, by which the farmers would suffer in a severe degree. At the Pier they might lie four or five days, or till the spring tide came again, which was 9 or 10 days.

He measured the draught of water at the Pier on the 9th May 1835, the tide flowing at 10, and alongside it was five feet, in the middle seven feet, and at the extremity seven feet five inches. Their vessels would not move under seven feet, and not under eight if there was any wind.

If the Pier had been made more to the eastward, they would have been given two feet more water; the Pier was decidedly put in the wrong place.

Thomas Pritchard said, he had been a pilot at Southend for 16 years, and was well acquainted with the water there; he described where he had brought in a vessel of 162 tons burthen, and said it must be an exceeding high tide if they found 12 feet of water on that shore. For the last three weeks no vessel drawing 10 feet of water could get into the harbour: the smallest of the **Messrs. Vandervord's** vessel would not be handled with confident in less than eight feet or eight feet two inches, the largest in nine feet of water: he should say that when they caught the harbour with nine feet of water once, they caught 20 times with not above six feet. If **Mr. Vandervord's** *Holy Oak* had been lying in the harbour all last week, there it would have no more floated in that water than he (witness) could fly. If he had gone in he must have stopped for sufficient water to float him out, and that was very uncertain.

In cross examination the witness said if **Mr. Vandervord's** barge had been built so as to draw less water, there was nothing to prevent their going to the Pier.

Mr King, of the Custom House, Leigh, was called, and after some objections to his being examined, said, he had some local knowledge of Southend; he should think that **Messrs. Vandervord's** barges might get to the harbour occasionally, but seldom; when in they might be delayed to his disadvantage. He thought a vessel of 160 tons might approach the Pier, but not get in to unload.

In cross-examination witness said occasionally a vessel might come in to load or unload; there was a crane fixed for the use of persons getting out goods.

Re-examined. He thought there was a great deal more water where **Messrs Vandervord's** barges unloaded. He thought that the Pier ought not to have been made where it was.

John Ferguson, a superannuated coal-meter, spoke to a vessel of 160 tons unloading opposite the Ship; such a vessel could not unload at the Pier.

Mr. Patterson said, the water on west side of the Pier was a foot or 14 inches deeper than in the harbour, and vessels, of the size of **Mr. Vandervord's** could load and unload there.

Mr Ferguson recalled. He thought the best place for a Pier would have been below the Ship.

Mr Knox then addressed the Magistrate in reply. It appeared to him the great fallacy on the other side was this, that they supposed when the Act was obtained the result would be the formation of a Harbour not Pier; and if it was intended the effect should that vessels were to be accommodated of a size that had never used it before, there would be some force in the arguments employed; but the whole object was to build a Pier, as was shown in the Preamble of the Act.

The Learned Gentleman proceeded to contend that the Company having done all that was required by the Act, and having formed a Pier that would enable vessels that could use the water, to load and unload at it, they were entitled to demand the dues. He had no doubt that it would be possible to make the Pier in a place more advantageous to the **Messrs. Vandervord**, but the question was, would it be more beneficial to the public. It was wrong to suppose that the Act had a mercantile object solely in view - for the accommodation of the bargemasters, - it was for the benefit of all persons resorting to that place, and with these terms the Company had complied.

The learned Gentleman went through the evidence at some length, and submitted that the Company being clearly entitled to the toll, the defendant must be convicted.

By permission of the Magistrate, **Mr. Price** then called **George Vandervord** to prove, that when **Mr. Patterson** went on board to seize, his authority was demanded.

Charles Brooks also spoke to what took place.

Mr. Patterson swore that his authority was not demanded; and **Eleazer Pepper**, who was with him, said he did not hear it.

Mr Disney said, the 85th section empowered the Company to make a Pier, and the same section described the kind of Pier they must make before they were entitled claim the dues: that Pier had been erected, and the simple question was to as the loadability or unloadability of the vessels. Now it appeared to him that it was meant for vessels capable of loading there, and that it was not meant to make it fit for large ships; it was clear the Pier was a benefit to place, and it appeared to him that if the defendant unloaded at the end of the Pier he would have considerable advantage, for it was in evidence that vessels of a larger burthen than this had unloaded there. Therefore, he had come to the conclusion which, however, he hoped would be revised elsewhere, for he should not like it all to depend upon his opinion —that on the construction of the Act the defendant must be convicted. He therefore convicted him in the penalty of the single duty for not giving an account on the days named; but on the cases of resistance, he was not sufficiently satisfied to give his judgement.

Mr. Knot then applied for costs, which it was stated amounted to about £25.

Mr. Disney granted costs to the extent of £20.

There was another information against **Mr. Vandervord**, brother of the last defendant, the hearing of which **Mr. Price** strongly urged should be postponed.

Mr Knot opposed the application, and after a long discussion the case was proceeded with.

The same witnesses were called as in the last case, to prove that goods had been loaded or unloaded on six occasions without any account been given.

Defendant was convicted in the same penalties as in the last case, and **Mr Disney** gave £5 costs.

There were two other information's which **Mr. Knox** said he would withdraw."

6. SOUTHEN PIER SALE/PURCHASE BY LOCAL BOARD 1874/1875
(Extracts and letters)

A public meeting of the owners of property and ratepayers, was called for Friday evening (30th October 1874) last, by Mr. G. Vandervord, the chairman of the board, in pursuance of a requisition signed by 20 ratepayers".

There is a debate about the exact details of the sale of Southend Pier. The local historian Benton, in his book *Southend and Sea, Historical Notes* written in 1909 states:

"In December 1873, the Pier was offered to the Local Board at £12,000; the net income being given as £550. The Board offered £10,000. The owners refused, and the Board had to pay £12,000. A large majority of the ratepayers signified their assent to the bargain.

But the proposed purchase of the pier was highly controversial.

Extracts from the *Chelmsford Chronicle* of 6th November 1874 reported,

PROPOSED PURCHASE SOUTHEND PIER BY THE LOCAL BOARD. STORMY MEETING - A POLL DEMANDED.

"For some days Southend has been in an unusual state of excitement consequent upon the proposal of the Local Board of Health to purchase the pier, and work it for the benefit of the town, instead of allowing it to remain, as present, a private speculation. A preliminary meeting was held last week, at which the subject was talked over, with the result that a public meeting of the owners of property and ratepayers, was called for Friday evening last, by **Mr. G. Vandervord**, the chairman of the board, in pursuance of a requisition signed by 20 ratepayers".

The meeting was preceded by the posting of large quantity of mural literature, those who oppose the scheme, principally the smaller ratepayers and watermen who consider the proposal an extravagant one, but whose statements received a smart handling at the meeting, which was rather noisy, the clamorous opponents preventing some of the remarks from being heard by more than one half of those present.

The meeting was held in the Public Hall. There was a large attendance, including a few ladies, ratepayers or otherwise in the gallery, where also one or two of the opposition sat.

Mr. Vandervord, by virtue of his official position as summoning and returning officer (as explained by **Mr. W. Gregson, jun.**, the clerk to the board) occupied the chair. He said he was pleased to see such a large attendance. He hoped they would seriously consider the question, like Englishmen, vote according to their best judgment. He would endeavour to obtain a fair hearing for each speaker, whether for against the proposal, and he asked for the support of the meeting in his endeavours to maintain order. [Applause,] The promoters had no personal feeling in the matter, beyond the desire to do what was best for the town, and would be glad to carry out the desires of the majority of the ratepayers.

That this meeting consents to the promotion by the Local Board, in the ensuing Session of Parliament, of a Bill or Act conferring on the Board the powers following (that is to say) to purchase the Southend Pier and all property, works, rights, powers, profits, and privileges appurtenant thereto; power to borrow the purchase money and monies required for necessary repairs, alterations, extensions, and other expenses on the security of the rates; power to carry on and work the undertaking; and such other powers as may be incidental to or requisite and proper in connection with the above objects or any them; and consents to the expenses in relation to promoting such bill being charged upon and paid out of the General District Rates.

Mr. Heygate seconded the motion, but before doing so he expressed the hope that **Mr. Smith**, having given expression to his own opinions [laughter] on a former occasion, would now quietly allow others to express theirs. (applause) and if **Mr. Smith** had anything further to advance he had no doubt the meeting would hear him. (Renewed plaudits). They were assembled on that most important occasion, because upon their conduct that night might on depend on whether the pier should be purchased for the benefit of the town or not.

The board had no power to apply for a bill without the ratepayers gave them authority, and if the authority were given the board would carry out the wishes of the ratepayers with as little expense as possible. It had been alleged that they were proposing to purchase a property which was in a very bad state of repair, and which would cost great deal to put into sound condition, and that the friends of the movement had exaggerated the danger the pier belonging to other people; they also averred that a part of the expense would fall upon the rates.

His own view, and that of his colleagues, were precisely on the contrary. He submitted first, that the pier was now offered at a price at which they could never hope it would be offered them again, because after its value had been publicly made known would never come into the market again at the same low price.

Secondly, they were sure that the Local Board could make more of the pier than anyone else could and could work it to the relieving of the rates because there was a large quantity of valuable land attached to it which could be utilised for public offices, without the expenditure of any money for other sites. (Hear, hear.)

And thirdly, they urged that the powers of the act under which the pier was at present held were very dangerous powers to be vested in a private body, and might be used as a sharp sword against the public, while if the powers were in the hands of the public authority the sword might be used for the protection of the town's interests. [Applause.]

Dwelling upon this latter point he pointed out the details of the bill under which the pier was originally constructed, showing that whereas, along the whole course of the Essex coast, from Tilbury Fort to Harwich, there was no place for the embarking or landing of troops, the government were anxious, without launching into the undertaking themselves, to grant such inducements as would lead others to invest capital in the project, and thirty-five years ago an act was passed which formed the germ of the present

He then read clauses from the act showing that there was power under it to exact a charge of 1s. 6d. for each passenger landing or embarking, which would put an end to all pleasuring if the power was put in force. There was an idea prevailing that boatmen were exempt, but they had only been exempted through the liberality of the authority holding the power.

He also read from the act to show that heavy tolls could be charged for goods and merchandise landed or embarked. These, he said, were fearful clauses, and he thought he had shown the edge of the sword which an enemy might make very oppressive to the inhabitants, but which the ratepayers might use for their own protection if they instructed the board to purchase the pier, and the powers under which it was governed.

It was the best investment he could recommend to the ratepayers, and he hoped they would give their representatives authority to secure it. (Renewed cheering).

Mr. Hy. Childs, a waterman, asked if the board could guarantee continued protection to the watermen before the purchase was effected. [Laughter.]

Mr. Heygate replied that of course they had no such power, but if the members the board did not treat the watermen properly after the purchase, they must turn them out. [Laughter and cheers.]

Mr. Childs: If you can see £10,000 worth in that pier why don't you buy it yourself? [Cheers.]

Mr. Heygate: I have had serious thoughts of buying it myself.

Mr. Childs: Ah, very serious. [Laughter, and cries of order."]

Mr. Heygate: I should be very sorry to impose upon you such tolls as I should be empowered to do, because I know it would bring such destruction upon the place that you would gladly appeal to the Local Board to help you.

The Chairman said he saw a member of the board present who was not with them at the former meeting. He did not know what **Mr. Arnold's** opinions were, but it was desirable to hear the opinions of all.

Mr. Arnold said he was a minority at the board. He had been described as the "factious minority." [Laughter.] But it did not always follow that the minority was wrong. They need not be frightened by the act of parliament which had been quoted from. The act was as old as the pier, and the pier was worn out. [Laughter.] There was no telling what it would cost to repair it, but they had seen a bill on the walls estimating the cost, and those figures he was ready to endorse. He could not recommend the purchase. Let those who had faith in it form themselves into a company and purchase it. (Applause.)

Mr. Mayes thought if they passed a vote of thanks to the chairman of the board for the efforts they had taken in investigating this matter they would do what was easiest and best. The board had doubtless been actuated by the best intentions, but it did not seem desirable that they should take any further steps. [Hear, hear.]

Mr. Berry asked if they were to understand from **Mr. Heygate's** speech that it was intended to lay out a large sum of money erecting new public offices?

Mr. Heygate explained that the act of parliament required the Local Board to have offices, and it had been found a difficult matter to procure them, the cost of a site being deterrent. They now had hired offices, but if they purchased the pier, the freehold land going with it would form a site, on which they could erect a respectable toll house, which would serve for offices also, and be an ornament to the town.

Mr. Palmer then rose amid plaudits to support the resolution. He inferred from the vast amount of printer's ink which had been displayed on the walls since their former meeting a great deal of interest had been excited upon this question. **Mr. Palmer** here referred to a handbill, which was a parody of the notice issued convening the meeting, to the effect that in compliance with a requisition signed by 250 "ignorant watermen" the writer gave notice that 'a meeting would be held," &c, for the purpose of protesting against the action of the Local Board in proposing to effect this purchase. **Mr. Palmer**, exhibiting the handbill, said his meaning had been wilfully perverted. When he used the words "ignorant watermen" on the previous occasion he did not of course mean that they were more ignorant than other people the ordinary sense of the term, but simply that they were ignorant to the wording of the act of parliament which had been quoted that night, and he appealed to the meeting, without fear of contradiction, to whether four-fifths of the assembly were not totally ignorant of the wording of those sections which had just been read. [Hear, hear.] Then it was said that no Local Board could enter into such contract on behalf of the ratepayers. Well, but the fact was that that meeting had been called for the very purpose of asking the ratepayers to consent to the board entering into such contract. [Hear, hear.]

Mr Palmer In opposition to this amateur guesswork, he would read to the meeting the estimate of an eminent firm of surveyors, Messrs. J. and A. E. Bull, of Charing Cross, who said in accordance with your request, we have carefully examined the condition and state of repair of the pier and other matters in connection therewith at Southend, and have also estimated the cost reinstate the same as follows, viz.:

1st. Thorough restoration. This includes certain improvements which we deem not only advisable to preserve the pier from decay, but in the long run a much, more economical outlay, and consists chiefly of coating the whole of the staging and landing with tar paving as this would add additional weight upon the carriages or bearers of the staging it will be necessary to truss the latter with iron rods, put intermediate cross bearers between the piles. These trusses are not only necessary to carry the additional weight of the paving but are required to render the staging safe even the present planking is renewed and preserved as originally laid. The distance, 26 feet, between the piles as present constructed is unsafe when large numbers of people are congregated at any particular point.

The other item of importance is to put spurs to all the piles from the shore end to within about 3,000 feet of the pier head; these are not absolutely necessary at present and may not on more minute examination be needed for several years to come, but we have included them in our estimate to insure the cost not exceeding the limits we quote.

The other items refer to renewing the defective and decayed works and tarring and painting the whole as previously done. The above we estimated at £3,588.

P.S. We have the offer of a contractor for the tar paving to execute this portion of the work, and guarantee to keep it in repair for three years.

2nd. Thorough restoration as above, to be extended over a period of five years. This, we estimate at the annual outlay of £790.

3rd. Immediate indispensable repair. This will consist of the trussed rods and bearers described in estimate No. 1, spurs those piles at present dangerous, removing all other defective and decayed works, tarring, and painting as previously done. Our estimate for this amounts to £1,500.

4th. Immediate and other necessary repairs for five years from present date. This will include the works stated in estimate No. 3. Also, additional spurs from time to time, and general repair. And we estimate the above at an annual outlay of £484.

Time does not permit us to enter minutely into matters of detail, but our estimates include them. Herewith we hand you the opinion of **Mr. Homer**, C.E., also of **Mr. Cooke**, contractor, in support our own. The former suggests that intermediate piles be driven on either side of the staging with the 26 feet bearings; this we propose to meet at a much less cost by using the truss rods and bearers, which we are satisfied will give ample security.

Mr. Palmer supplemented this by reading the report **of Mr. Homer**, who estimated that a thorough restoration could be effected for £3.350.

The contents of these documents met with marked approval. The speaker then appealed to the meeting whether they were not perfectly satisfied when the largest ratepayers the owners of property such as **Mr. Baxter, Mr. Scott, Mr Louth**, and himself and others, were much more deeply interested than the man who only paid £50 a year rental for a house in Cliff Town Parade. [Laughter and cheers.]

Mr. Frost: I rise to order. I must ask Mr. Palmer to refrain from personalities. [Confusion.]

The Chairman: I must ask you to sit down. [Hear, hear.)

Mr. Frost: Mr. Palmer is becoming personal I live at Cliff Town Parade. [Laughter.]

The Chairman: I call for order.

Mr. Frost: I won't be put down. Mr. Palmer, by alluding to me as living in Cliff Town Parade, won't put me down.

Mr. Palmer: Do you occupy the whole of the premises in Cliff Town Parade [Laughter.]

Mr. Frost: I won't be put down. That is a very invidious remark.

Mr. Palmer: I believe there are more houses than one in Cliff Town Parade, but I am perfectly willing, if the cap fits, that **Mr. Frost** should put it on and wear it. [Laughter, cheers, and cries of " time."] What, are you ashamed of your own bill? If you are I will sit down. [Cries of " Go on.")

At the last meeting some gentlemen seemed to feel great sympathy with **Mr. Gregson** the clerk, because he could not reply. **Mr. Cranfield** (who spoke from the gallery at the other end of the hall) here "repudiated" something, but it was impossible hear what.

Mr. Palmer: Mr. Cranfield had put down in his estimate an additional salary of £100 a year to the clerk for superintending the pier estate. He should only say to this, that there was no intention to create new offices, and that it was firmly believed that by adopting a proper system of checking they could manage without any extra help, and by paying the clerk the same amount of remuneration as at present the work could be done. (Hear, hear.) But if **Mr. Cranfield** and his fellow ratepayers thought

Mr. Gregson would be really entitled to more remuneration, of course **Mr. Gregson** would not be unwilling to receive it. [Laughter.]

Then, as to the next item, £360, for salaries and expenses of horse, that sum ought to include also the cost of ordinary repairs, as the books would show.

Mr. Cranfield: It does not. You don't know what you have been reading. You ought to go to an evening school. ("Order, order.")

Mr. Palmer was glad of this observation, because there was something in **Mr. Cranfield's** estimate which showed the necessity of some instruction in the matter of arithmetical calculation. He put down £16,700 as necessary to be borrowed and repaid, and he put the repayment at £1,600 a year, whereas if he calculated it at 4 per cent, he must find he had made a mistake.

Then **Mr. Cranfield** wound up with the startling conclusion that £1,205 would have to be taken out of the pockets of the ratepayers to pay for this undertaking. This he (**Mr. Palmer**) gave his most emphatic contradiction. The statement was as false as the whole document was fabulous. [Hear, hear.]

Mr. Cranfield: That's rather strong, sir. (Laughter.)

Mr. Palmer proceeded to show what the real figures were, and said the figures from which he had made his calculations were open to the test of any ratepayer.

The board proposed to borrow the money required, £14,000, for 30 years, at 4 per cent., which would cost £812 annually. The average expenditure for the past four years was £460; the estimated net revenue was £962, and this would give annual profit of £150 to the ratepayers. [Applause] But they were prepared go further than this, because taking the past three months, a pretty fair criterion as to what might be done, they found that instead profit, providing for the working expenses, payment of interest, and repairs, the whole thing might be worked and paid for, leaving a balance to the ratepayers of £486. [Cheers.]

These were statements which he made, and challenged contradiction. He did not found this upon a mere amateur opinion of his own, but upon the books of the company, and the estimates of eminent surveyors and engineers, and considered that one fact was worth a dozen mere statements. [Applause.] He insisted that it was the duty of the town to have possession of its own pier, and then the boatmen and the public could be protected, as it was the wish of the board to protect them. [Renewed plaudits.]

Mr. Cranfield said he considered that any man who told him that statements he made were false was not worth replying to. [Laughter and cheers.] As to **Mr. Heygate's** speech, it was like some of the beer they drank now-a-days, it had too much sugar in it. [Laughter.] The opinions he had published with respect to the pier were not his own. He **Mr Cranfield** had consulted one of the most eminent engineers in London upon the matter. [Cries of "Name."] There was not one item upon that paper, but he could take his oath to its truth.

Mr. Cranfield, however, refused give the name, and when pressed to do so said he did not mean submit to any dictation, a remark which was condemned general hissing.

Mr. Mayes said that the figures **Mr. Palmer** had produced sounded very clear and plain, but there might arise accidents or contingencies which could not at present be foreseen, and they might be called upon to pay expensive damages.

Mr. Hudson If the great majority of the ratepayers thought the pier, in its present rotten state, should be purchased, well and good, but if a company was started for building a new pier, they had better put their hands into their pockets for a structure which they knew something about than for one they knew nothing about.

Mr. Lawton said there was such a wide difference between the opinions expressed that he should be glad if Mr. Scott, a man of great practical experience, would give his opinion with respect the condition of the pier.

Mr. Scott said he was of opinion that the pier ought to be in the possession of the local authorities, but he did not consider himself competent to give an opinion as to its condition.

The meeting having been protracted, and there having been frequent cries of "divide," **the Chairman** asked if any other gentleman wished to speak to the resolution, but he received no reply.

Mr. Dowsett: There are many gentlemen here who are not ratepayers. How do you propose to take the vote?

The Chairman: Will those gentlemen who are not ratepayers retire from the room: I shall be much obliged to them if they will.

There was a large exodus of non-ratepayers, during which **Mr. Frost** handed in a demand for a poll, on behalf of the opponents of the purchase, the Chairman told him could not receive such a demand until after the voting.

The question being put, there appeared about 50 hands for the resolution and between 60 and 70 against it, and **the Chairman** declared the resolution not carried. **Mr. Baxter** and **Mr. Woosnam** then demanded poll, on behalf of the board, of which public notice will be given."

But the controversy continued. The *Southend Standard* of 13th November 1874. It included the republishing of a letter of protest about the purchasing of the pier by **William Cranfield** and **Thomas Arnold**. William Cranfield lived at 2 Whitegate Villas and was a corn miller. He was a member of Southend Local Board, and a member of the Finance Committee. He was very active in Southend affairs. **Thomas Arnold** was a farmer who had Thames Farm. He was also a member of Southend Local Board. He was active in Southend.

SOUTHEND PIER.

"To the Editor of the " Southend Standard."

Sir,—The following copy of a letter may interest the rate-payers of Southend at the present time. "Southend, May 8th, 1874.

To William Gregson, Esq.

Dear Sir,—We, the undersigned members of the Southend Local Government Board, request that before you proceed to send the contract signed by four members of the Board to **Mr. Wagstaff** relating to the purchase of Southend Pier by the Board, to call a meeting of the Board and explain in what part of Local Government Act or Acts you find authority for advising the Board to take the proceedings they are about to take under your advice, and for which you are and will be held responsible and which proceedings we protest against as being illegal and foreign to the office of the Board, and leading to an illegal expenditure of the rate-payers money and for which expenditure we will in no way be held responsible and entirely repudiate.

We are, Dear Sir, Yours respectfully,

William. CRANFIELD, Thomas. ARNOLD.

The meeting was called and met and **Mr. Gregson** admitted he had no authority for the advice given to the Board. **Mr. Cranfleld** proposed that the letter should be copied into the minute book. **Mr. Arnold** seconded it; the other four members opposed it. **Mr. Cranfield** then proposed that. as the Board refused to allow the letter to be entered in extenso, that the letter should be kept as a Board paper and preserved as such, this was carried and may be read by any ratepayer who may take the trouble to go to the office and read it. The ratepayers do not seem to understand that they have a perfect right to inspect and copy any paper or book that relates to the business of the Board, in fact all the papers and books are their own, and only under the care of the Board. The contract to buy the pier was only signed by four members, and no contract is a legal one unless signed by five. They had never seen the deed of conveyance from the Eastern Counties Railway Company to Mr. Brassey and others, but consented to take it *Nolens, Volens* (this means whether a person wants something or not), whatever restrictions it may contain. Whoever heard of such a way of doing business before.

I am, Sir, yours respectfully,

Thos. ARNOLD

7. 1875 PARLIAMENTARY ENABLING BILL APPLICATION

From *Southend Standard and Essex Weekly Advertiser* –
Friday 13 November 1874

In Parliament—Session 1875.

SOUTHEND LOCAL BOARD (Purchase of Pier & c. at Southend – *Provisions for vesting same and all the Powers of the Acts relating thereto the Local Board—Power to Local Board to hold and maintain Pier—To levy tolls—To purchase and dispose of lands—Change of name of District of Local Board and Town—Provisions with reference to landing and carting animals and goods in district—Application of Funds—Additional borrowing powers and power to debenture stock—Dissolution of Southend Pier Company—Other powers—Incorporation Amendment repeal and re-enactment of Acts.)*

NOTICE is hereby given that application is intended to be made to Parliament in the ensuing Session by the Local Board for the district of Southend in the County of Essex (hereinafter called "the Local Board") for leave to bring in a Bill for the following or some of the following among other purposes (that is to say)—

1.-To authorise the Local Board to purchase and acquire and the Owners of the Pier at Southend (hereinafter called 'the Owners.) to sell and transfer to the Local Board or otherwise to provide for the vesting in the Local Board the Pier at Southend all the lands and easements Southend and all the lands easements hereditments buildings works plant machinery apparatus chattels and effects belonging thereto or connected therewith to all the estate and property (real and personal) of of what nature or kind soever and all the rights powers privileges and authorities now belonging to or vested in or exercised and enjoyed by the Owners with respect to the said undertaking including all the rights powers privileges and authorities conferred by the Acts (Local) of 10 Geo. 4, cap. 49 and 5 and '6 Wm. 4, cap. 90, relating to the undertaking o otherwise and whether with reference to the purchase of lands the construction of works the levying of tolls duties and or otherwise howsoever upon such terms and conditions for such price and consideration as may have been or may hereafter be agreed upon or as shall be prescribed by the Bill and upon such transfer and vesting to authorise the Local Board to hold work maintain and use the said Pier and Undertaking and to have exercise and enjoy perform and fulfil all the rights powers privileges authorities and obligations conferred or imposed by the said Acts of 10 Geo. 4, cap. 49, and 5 and 6 Wm. 4, cap. whether with reference to the construction renewal maintenance and extension of said pier and undertaking the sale of lands and other property the levying of tolls rates duties and charges or otherwise howsoever.

2. To authorise the Local Board and the owners to enter into and carry into effect agreements for or with reference to such sale purchase transfer and vesting and to sanction and confirm any agreement already made or which prior to the passing of the Bill may be made for or with reference thereto.

3. To authorise the Local Board from time to time to maintain alter renew enlarge extend and improve the Pier and the works and conveniences connected therewith and from tune to time to construct and maintain additional works and conveniences for the purposes of the said undertaking.

4. To enable the Local Board to levy tolls, rate, duties and charges for the use of the Pier and other works and conveniences connected therewith and for landing and embarking Passengers animals minerals goods and other traffic and for all or any of the purposes authorised by the said Acts of 10 Geo. 4. cap. 49, and 5 and 6Wm. 4, cap. 90, or either of those Acts to alter the tolls rates duties and charges now levied for the use of the Pier and other the purposes aforesaid and to confer vary or extinguish exemptions from this payment of all or any or such tolls rates or duties and to confer vary or extinguish other rights privileges and exemptions

5. To empower the Local Board from time to time to purchase by agreement and take on lease and to take grants of easements over additional lands and houses for all or any of the purposes of the Bill and for the general purposes of the Local Board and to sell let or Otherwise dispose of all or any lands or other property purchased or acquired by them under the powers of the Bill and which may not eventually be required for the purposes thereof.

6. To change or provide for the changing the name of the District of the Local Board and of the Town of Southend.

7. To make provision for regulating the landing and carting of animals, goods, merchandise, manure, and other matters and things within and through the district of the Local Board and to enable the Local Board to make and enforce bye-laws rules and regulations with reference thereto and to impose penalties for the breach thereof:

8. To authorise the Local Board to apply to the purposes of the Bill or any of them any funds moneys rates or rents now belonging to them or which they are now or by the Bill may be authorised to raise or which may come into their possession in exercise of the Powers which either now are or from time to time shall be conferred upon them and to authorise the Local Board to raise additional funds for all or any of the purposes of the Bill by borrowing on the security of the Pier and of the Property to be vested In the Local Board and of the tolls rates and duties now leviable or to be levied or created by or to arise under the powers of the Bill or by mortgage of the General District rate or general district fund account or by bond or by way of annuity or by debenture stock charged on the rates and revenues of the Local Board or be all or some of the aforesaid Means and to make provision for the repayment of the sums borrowed or raised under the Bill and to define and declare the funds revenues and property, liable to such debts and upon which the same shall attach or be charged.

9. To confer upon the Local Board and the owners and all other necessary parties all such powers, rights, authorities, and privileges which are or may become necessary or expedient for carrying the powers of the Bill into execution. To vary and extinguish all powers, rights, authorities, and privileges inconsistent with or which would in any manner impede or interfere with the carrying into complete effect any of the objects and purposes of the Bill and to confer other rights, authorities, and privileges.

10. To provide if need be for the dissolution of the Southend Pier Company and the winding up of their affairs.

11. To incorporate with the Bill or to re-enact with such variations, modifications and exceptions as may be thought expedient and make applicable to the Local Board and their Pier undertaking all or some of the provisions of the Lands clauses consolidation Acts 1845, 1860 and 1869 and the Harbours Docks and Piers Clauses Act 1847 or parts thereof respectively and any Other Acts or parts of Acts that may be necessary for effecting the objects of the Bill.

12. And it is also proposed so far as it may be necessary or expedient for all or any of the purposes of the Bill to alter amend extend or enlarge and if need be to repeal and re-enact either in extenso or by reference and with such variations modifications and exceptions as may be deemed expedient all or some of the powers and provisions of the local and personal Acts of Parliament following—that is to say-10 Geo. 4 cap. 49 and 6 and 6 Win. 4 cap. 90 and all other Acts (if any) which may relate to the Pier or be affected by the objects of the Bill.

13. And notice is hereby also given that printed copies of the Bill will be deposited in the Private Bill Office of the House of Commons on or before the 21st day of December next.

Dated this 12th day of November 1874

WILLIAM GREGSON, Jun,
Southend, Solicitor:
TOOGOOD and BALL,
16, Parliament Street, Westminster; Parliamentary Agents.

Bibliography

Benton, Philip   *A History of the Rochford Hundred Rochford:*
A. Harrington 1867

Bride, H, N, Ald   *Southend Pier & its Story, Southend Corporation*

Burrows, John Wm   *Southend Pier and its Story 1829-1835-1935* John
                        Burrows and Son, 1936

Burrows John Wm   *Southend on Sea, Historical Notes, Burrows and*
                        Son, 1909

Easdown, Martin   Southend Pier, Tempus 2007

Everritt ,Sylvia   *Southend: Seaside Holiday,* Phillimore, 1980

Gordon Dee   *The Secret History of Southend-on-Sea,*
                        The History Press, 2014

Granville Dr Augustus *The Spas of England and Principle Sea Bathing*
                        Places, 1841

King, Tom and   *The Southend Story, A Town and its People*
Furbank, Kevin   Southend Standard, 1991

Pollitt, William   *The Spas of England and principle sea bathing*
                        places 1760 – 1860, Southend-on-Sea Public
                        Libraries and Museum Committee,1939

Pollitt, William *The Rise of Southend,* John H Burrows and Son Ltd
                        1957

Rayment, David C   *A-Z of Southend: Places-People-History*
                        Amberley Publishing Limited, 2019

Shepherd, E,W   *The Story of Southend Pier,* Egon Publishing, 1979

Strutt, William   *The History of Old Southend Pier, (1829-1838)*
                        As Portrayed in the correspondence of Major-
                        General Goodday Strutt

Tawke, Augusta   *Hunting Recollections, 1911*

Tawke, Augusta   *Bulwood Hall, Hockley, Rochford,* 1911

Tawke , Augusta   *Recollections of Southend-on-Sea and*
                        Neighbourhood 1855-1912
                        Republished by Peter C Brown 1915
                        Thames River, The Thames and Its Story, From the
                        Cotswolds to the Nore 1906

Yearsley, Ian   *A History of Southend*, Phillimore & Co. Ltd, 2001

Online resources

www.archive.org

www.british-history.ac.uk

www.southendtimeline.com

The National Archives
http://blog.nationalarchives.gov.uk

Essex Records Office
http://seax.essexcc.gov.uk/

https://www.findagrave.com/

https://www.britannica.com/

https://www.collinsdictionary.com

https://rnli.org/find-my-nearest/lifeboat-stations/southend-on-sea-lifeboat-station/station-history-southend-on-sea

https://www.britishnewspaperarchive.co.uk/

https://www.rochfordtown.com/historic-rochford/books-and-research/

www.wikipedia.org

www.wikitree.com

https://pubwiki.co.uk

Index

About the Author

Marion Pearce has lived in Southend-on-Sea since she was a small child. She was the co-founder of SKIPP, Saxon King in Priory Park and spent many years campaigning for the return and display of the Saxon King exhibits, which are now displayed in Southend Museum.

Marion believes Southend has a wonderful opportunity to regenerate itself through ancient history. Marion has been active in getting the historic fountain repaired at Prittlewell Square, which is Southend's oldest park. She has campaigned too on the 14th Century Southchurch Hall, which was put on the "heritage at risk" list as well as keeping a watchful eye on the Crowstone, the Royal Hotel, the Kursaal and of course Southend Pier.

Marion is the author of *Milton, Chalkwell, and the Crowstone*, now available from bookshops and online. Besides being an author of local history books, Marion has written the following available from online suppliers,

The Roman Calendar, *explores the origins of our calendar and dates back to the days of ancient Rome. The festivals and various celebrations are described, from the wild excesses of the Lupercalia to the gentler pastoral Floralia and Ambarvalia, the Roman zest for life shines through their year. The whole of the Roman world can be found in the chronology of time and how they related to their God's and Goddesses, their mythology, their sports, harvests, work and play.*

Celtic Sacrifice, *where you enter the world of the Celts, a world of magic, shape-shifting, sorcery and divination, a world where legend and fact are mixed, where the physical world and the Otherworld blend in heroism, rituals and rites. Combining sources from mythology and archaeology with eye-witness accounts from the period, this book presents a fascinating picture of Celtic religion, worship, and deity and investigates the significance of trees, animals, bones, burial practices, kingship and cults of the head and the dead.*

and *Gods of the Vikings,* *which traces the Norse gods who are as vivid and powerful as the rugged elemental landscapes they ruled over. It sets the major Norse gods like Odin, Thor, Loki, Tyr, Baldur, Freya and Frigg into a context of both time and place, telling their tales in a unique manner and through doing so she introduces numerous other gods, giants, heroes, dwarves and monsters from the Norse myths and legends.*

Porters
The Mayor's House
in Southend-on- Sea

One time home of successive generations of the Heygate family

Essex Hundred Publications publishes a range of Essex centered local history books. By Essex we mean not just the county of Essex as it is today but also the areas of Essex that have been absorbed into London since 1965.

The company also distributes a range of local history books from other publishers and has a large portfolio of Essex images.

Essex Hundred authors are also happy to give talks on the subjects published.

For further details check out www.essex100.com or e-mail ask@essex100.com

Selected titles available from
Essex Hundred Publications

Milton, Chalkwell and the Crowstone
By Marion Pearce
Milton Hamlet has sunk into oblivion, but still to be found are traces of the 'middle town' between Leigh-on-Sea and Southchurch. Chalkwell is a thriving residential area which has its roots in the large estates of the Victorian era and the Crowstone has been a landmark in the Thames estuary for nearly eight hundred years.
ISBN 9781739931605

Once Upon a time in Southend (and District)
Edited by Andrew Summers
Cartoons are one of the most popular staples of newspapers. The cartoonists' genius lies not just with drawing skills but their ability to bring together contemporary and historical events in a single image.
ISBN 9780993108396

FAMOUS ESSEX AUTHORS You have never heard of
By Dee Gordon
There are some names that you will have heard of and literally dozens of names that have been, sadly, forgotten over time. You may recognise some book titles. Some of the romance writers featured may not have famous names or even famous "titles" but they were prolific and popular. Earlier generations of writers set the stage for those current Essex writers that feature on the bestseller lists and it has also been important for Essex to include big guns such as Austen, Shakespeare and Dickens, however tenuous the links in such cases!
ISBN 9781739931629

The Rise, Fall and Rise of Horse Racing in Chelmsford
By David Dunford
In the 18th and 19th centuries Chelmsford Races, held on Galleywood Common, were the most eagerly anticipated event in the Essex social calendar. They had something for everyone: the aristocracy could flaunt their wealth and power, the working classes enjoyed a rare day off and crooks and conmen fleeced the unwary.
ISBN 9781739931612

BUFFALO'S BILL'S WILD WEST
by David Dunford
The First Reality Show in Essex revealing the extraordinary story of Buffalo Bill, his Wild West show and what happened when they came to Essex in the early 1900s.
ISBN 9780993108389

The RIDDLE OF BOUDICA
By Andrew Summers
Explores the 'facts' of the rebellion as far is known and examines the resultant heritage, legacy and mythology which has grown up around it.
ISBN 9780993108334

BATTLEFIELD ESSEX
John Debenham and Andrew Summers
An account of 2000 years of conflict in Essex.
Some have been violent bloody battles but also many didn't
involve the loss of life. Although fought with passion and hyped in the media of the day into 'battles' and the term has since stuck.
ISBN 9780993108341

THE ESSEX HUNDRED HISTORIES
John Debenham and Andrew Summers
From the Roman sacking of Colchester to Ford's modern day wind turbines each chapter reflects the diversity of the county as well as showing the role Essex has played in the nation's development.
ISBN: 9780993108310

MAGNA CARTA IN ESSEX
John Debenham and Andrew Summers
Essex barons were at the forefront of those who pushed hard for the Magna Carta, with Robert Fitzwalter, Lord of Dunmow appointed their leader. Yet within three months of the charter being sealed England was at war and Essex racked by conflict.
ISBN 9780993108303 £7.99

THE NUMBERS HAD TO TALLY
by Kazimierz Szmauz
A World War II Extraordinary Tale of Survival
ISBN: 9780955229572

Due Autumn 2025

ONCE IN ESSEX, NOW IN LONDON
Essex before 1965 had clearly defined natural borders, the River Stour to the north, the North Sea to the east, the Thames to the south and the River Lea to the west. These borders were already established when England became a United Kingdom under the rule of King Alfred over 1000 years ago. They remained largely intact until the creation of the Greater London Council in 1965.
John Debenham, David Dunford and Andrew Summers
ISBN 9781739931636

DIGITAL EDITIONS AVAILABLE

Essex Farm
The Numbers Had to Tally
L33 and other stories from WWI

Essex Hundred Publications

Books written, designed and printed in Essex.
Available from bookshops, book wholesalers,
direct from the publisher or
online www.essex100.com